GAUTENG

JOHANNESBURG,

DISCO

CW01066858

RESEARCHED, DEVELOPED
AND CREATED BY JACANA

Witwatersrand National Botanical Garden

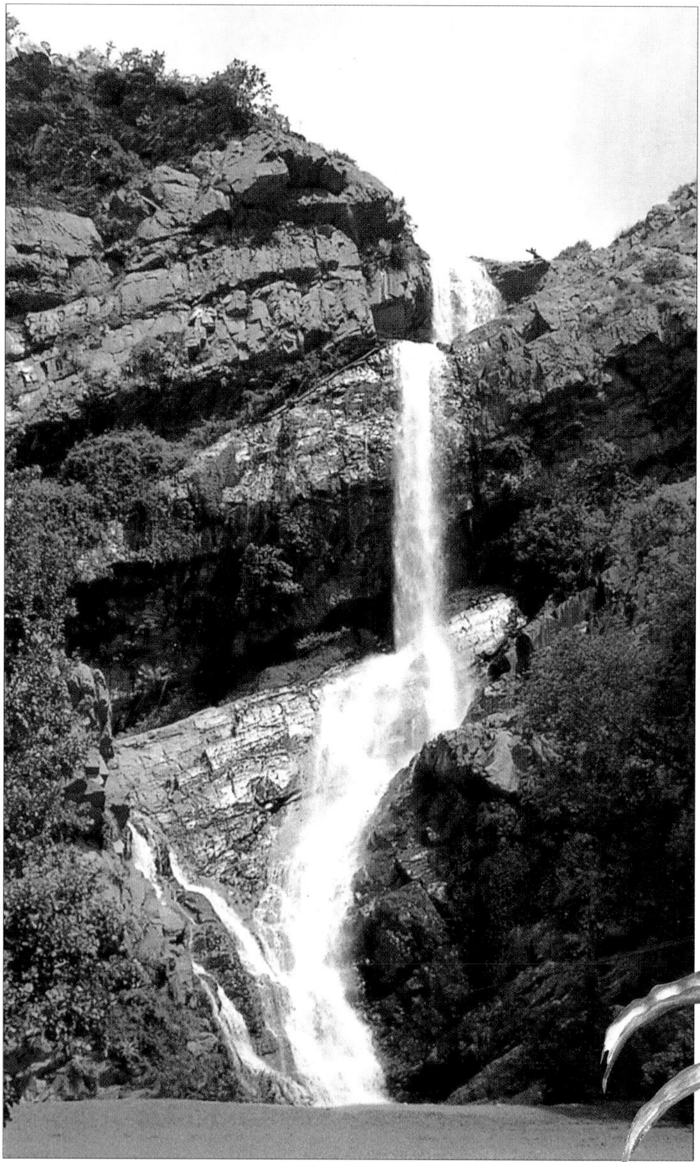

The Witwatersrand Natio Botanical Garden (NBG is set in an incredibly beaut spot. Its 200 metre high clif pierced by the Witpoortjie Waterfall, form the centrepi of the Garden. The Witwatersrand NBG is the fastest growing of eight botanical gardens belonging to the National Botanical Institute, based at Kirstenbo in Cape Town.

The Garden is almost 300 ha size, with over 30 ha under intensive cultivation, using exclusively South African pla

The Witpoortjie Waterfall

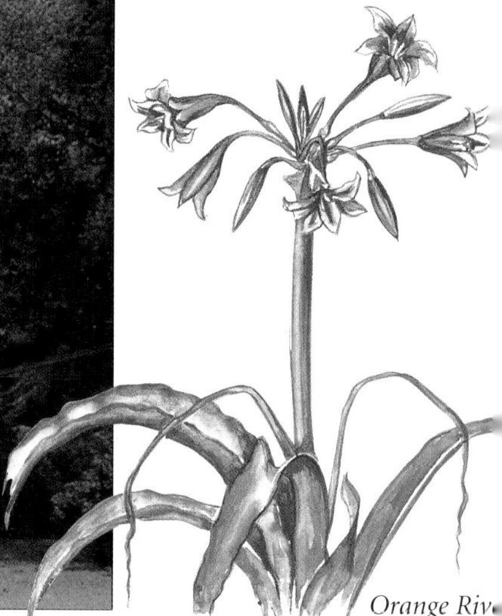

Orange Riv
(see pa

ıe cultivated area includes a cycad garden, succulent garden, water garden, fern ail, arboretum, Sasol Dam and wetland area, and the newly developed water-wise :monstration garden. In addition, there are a number of short walks and trails to : done in both the cultivated and natural portions of the garden. The JCI eological Trail has recently been developed and gives visitors the opportunity walk along the ridge, and also to learn something about the fascinating geology the area.

The larger portion of the Garden, which runs along the Roodekrans Ridge, is maintained as a nature reserve. The natural vegetation of the area consists of a mosaic of grassland and savannah, with dense bush in kloofs and along streams. Over 600 species of flowering plants, 230 species of birds (including a magnificent breeding pair of Black Eagles), as well as a number of reptiles and small mammals occur here naturally.

The Bankenveld Branch of the Botanical Society organise numerous events in the Garden to raise money for the Garden Development Fund. These events include Sunday picnic concerts, biannual indigenous plant sales and environmental courses.

Monarch
,
e 57)

Spotted Aloe
(see page 56)

;eneral Information and Facilities

'he Garden is open every day, including weekends and public holidays. The hours are from 8h00 – 17h00, with the exit gates closing at 18h00. A nominal entrance fee is payable. Senior itizens get free entrance on Tuesdays. Botanical Society members and children under 6 years old ıre allowed free entrance.

'he Restaurant is situated in the shade of two magnificent White Stinkwood trees, and serves ›reakfasts, lunches and teas.

ɜuided tours can be arranged around the Garden. These tours are led by volunteers who have ›een trained by the education officer at the Garden. In addition to general guided tours, an :xcellent schools programme is running in the Garden.

There is an attractive curio shop with a wide range of mementos and books with a southern \frican theme. The shop is open from 08h00 – 16h20 during the week, and from)8h00 – 17h00 on weekends and public holidays.

Contact Details

Witwatersrand National Botanical Garden
End of Malcolm Rd, Poortview, Roodepoort
Tel (011) 958-1750
Fax (011) 958-1752
Email witsnbg@mweb.co.za

ragonfly
:e page 57)

Star Flower
(see page 55)

The Transvaal Museum's sandstone facade is a familiar Pretoria lar

TRANSVAAL MUSEUM

The 'tourism' concept is generally associated with faraway and exotic places, and also with the cos involved in annually converting one's everyday existence to that of a tourist at leisure. For obvi reasons, the majority of tourist and field guides deal with the environment or the fauna and/or flor politically demarcated areas. In the previous provincial dispensation, the eco-tourism potential of t Greater Johannesburg/Pretoria area was hopelessly overshadowed by more famous destinations suc the Drakensberg mountains, the Kruger and Kalahari Gemsbok National Parks. As such, Gauteng province and its immediate surrounds remained unappreciated.

To the best of my knowledge this book is the first to introduce the eco-tourism potential of this are South Africa. It gives the visitor an overview of outdoor opportunities within a radius of two hours of the major centres. It furthermore provides easy and interesting reading on the more obvious anir and plant life, as well as ancient geological and historical features of the area. It is wonderful to disc that at minimal expense, I could spend every weekend and in some instances every day, exploiting t wide variety of activities offered in Johannesburg and beyond.

One such area which comes to mind is the world-renowned Sterkfontein Valley, where the fossil evidence for the origin of mankind, as well as the very first tools made by our predecessors, have be found.

Gauteng is indeed rich in biodiversity, and it has remarkable geological features, such as the massive Witwatersrand and the Soutpan meteor crater, begging discovery and appreciation. Those who bene from this book will agree that Gauteng's tourism and recreational potential is hopelessly under-estimated. I have no doubt that **Discover the Magic – Gauteng** will help to elevate the tourist potent this area to its rightful status.

Dr IL Rautenbach, Director
TRANSVAAL MUSEUM

Contents

Sunrise Scene - Introduction 2

Map 1 - South Gauteng (General) 4

Map 2 - North Gauteng (General) 6

Map 3 - South Gauteng (Specific) 8

Map 4 - North Gauteng (Specific) 10

Places to Visit and Things to Do 12

Land and Climate 28

Fish, Amphibians and Reptiles 42

Plants and Insects 50

Birds 72

Mammals 84

Human History 94

Human Impact 110

Night Scene - Conclusion 114

Index 116

Acknowledgements 121

Notes 122

Sunrise Scene

Dawn breaks on a cold Highveld winter's morning, and a mighty city stretches and wakens. It is the largest, inland development in the world not founded on a major river.

It has taken little more than a hundred years for Gauteng's great sprawling development of industry and urbanisation, home to many millions of people, to cover what was once little more than grassland.

Here, indeed, is a city of contrasts. Its story began with gold and greed. Its history encompasses untold suffering and inhumanity, and yet today it is the economic powerhouse of southern Africa, and the home to a remarkable and thriving democracy.

The city's glittering future jostles uneasily with its legacy of poverty and injustice. The warmth of its people, with their fascinating cultural differences, united by a common desire to build a better future, give Gauteng its strong sense of identity, and its irrepressible sense of hope.

Just as the cold, dry and brown Highveld winters give way to the lush, green, warmth of summer, and the parched earth is nourished by turbulent rainstorms, so too Gauteng thrives on the promise of a better tomorrow.

Sunrise over Gauteng

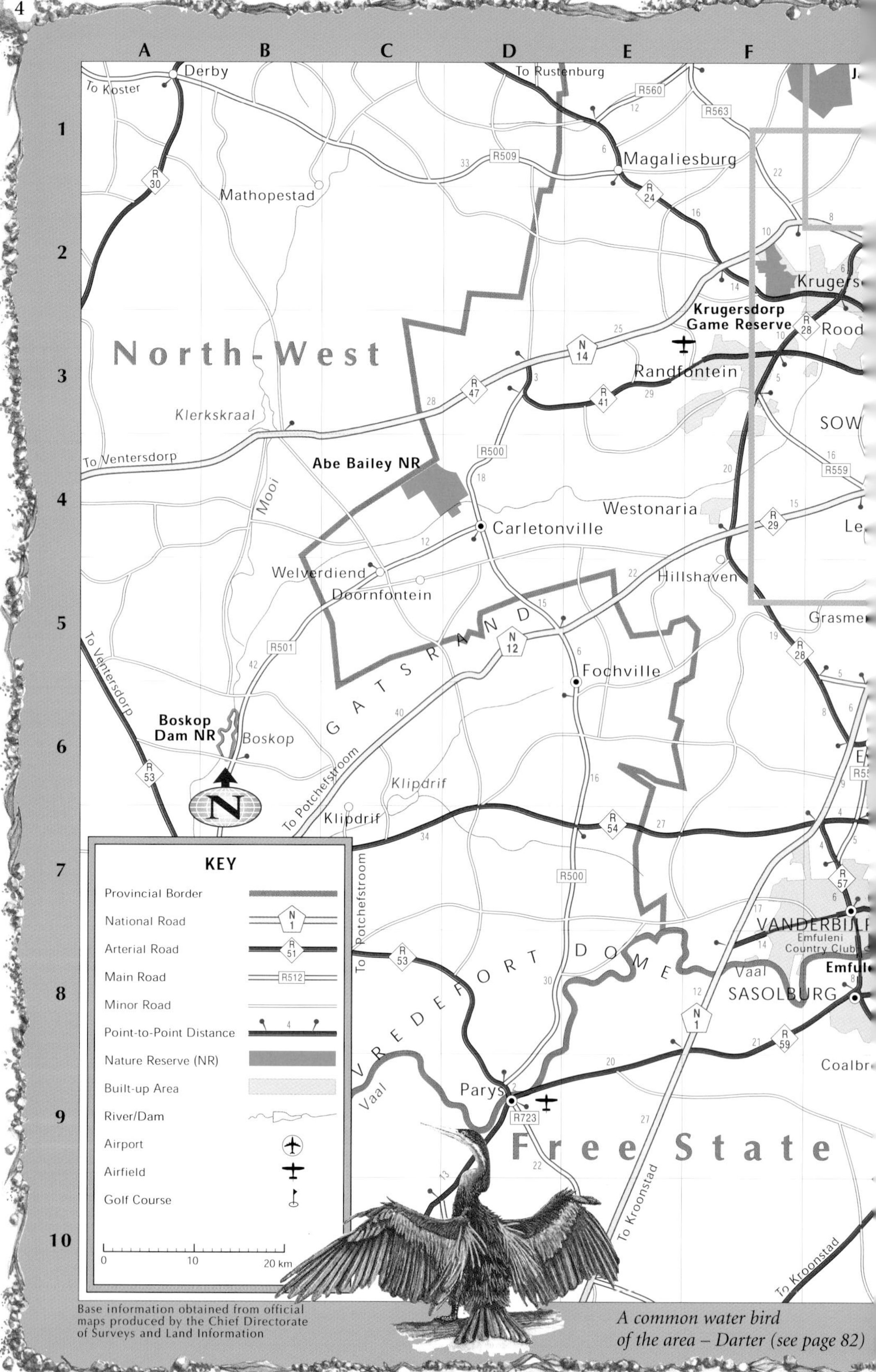

Base information obtained from official maps produced by the Chief Directorate of Surveys and Land Information

A common water bird of the area – Darter (see page 82)

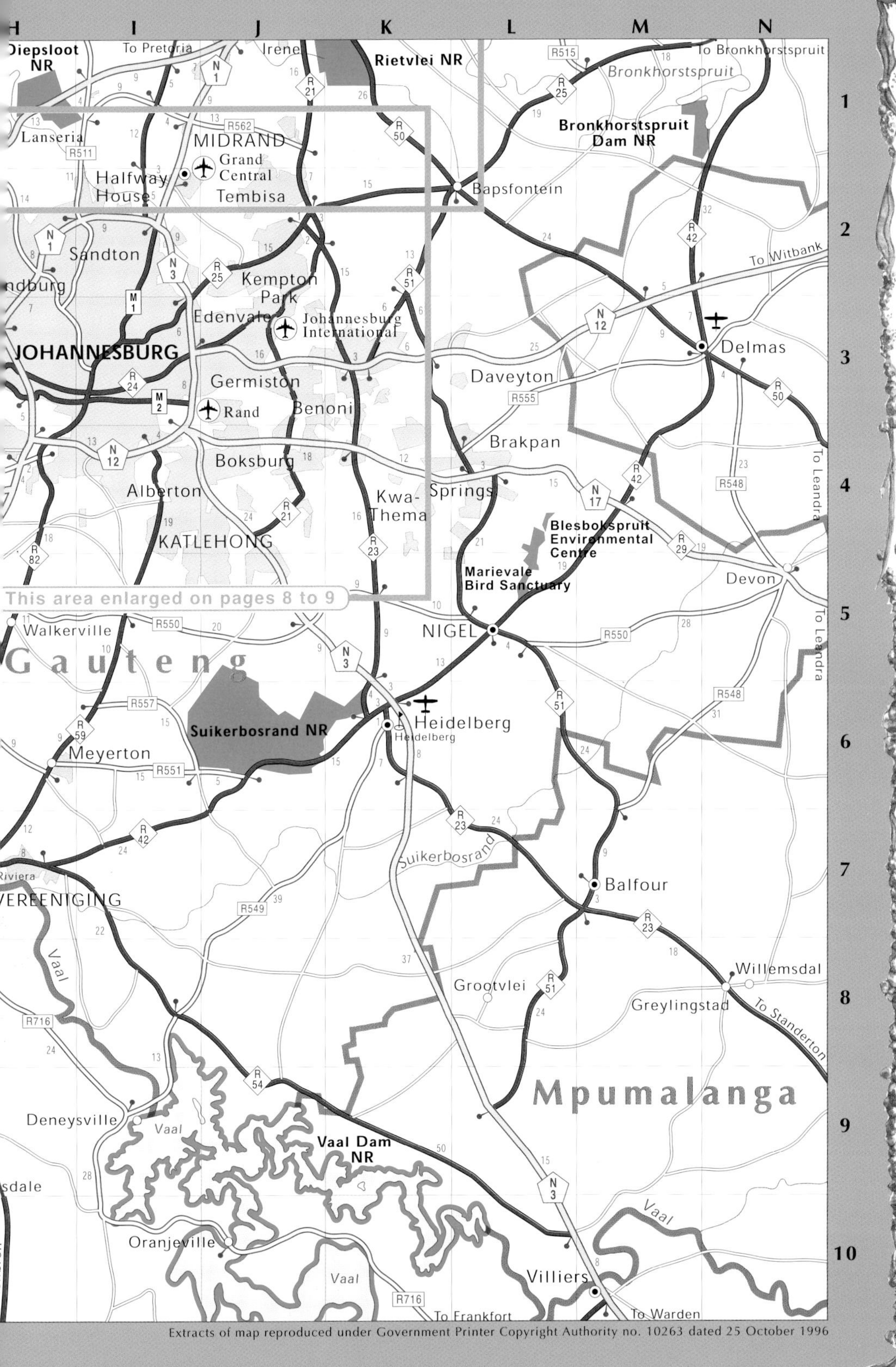

Extracts of map reproduced under Government Printer Copyright Authority no. 10263 dated 25 October 1996

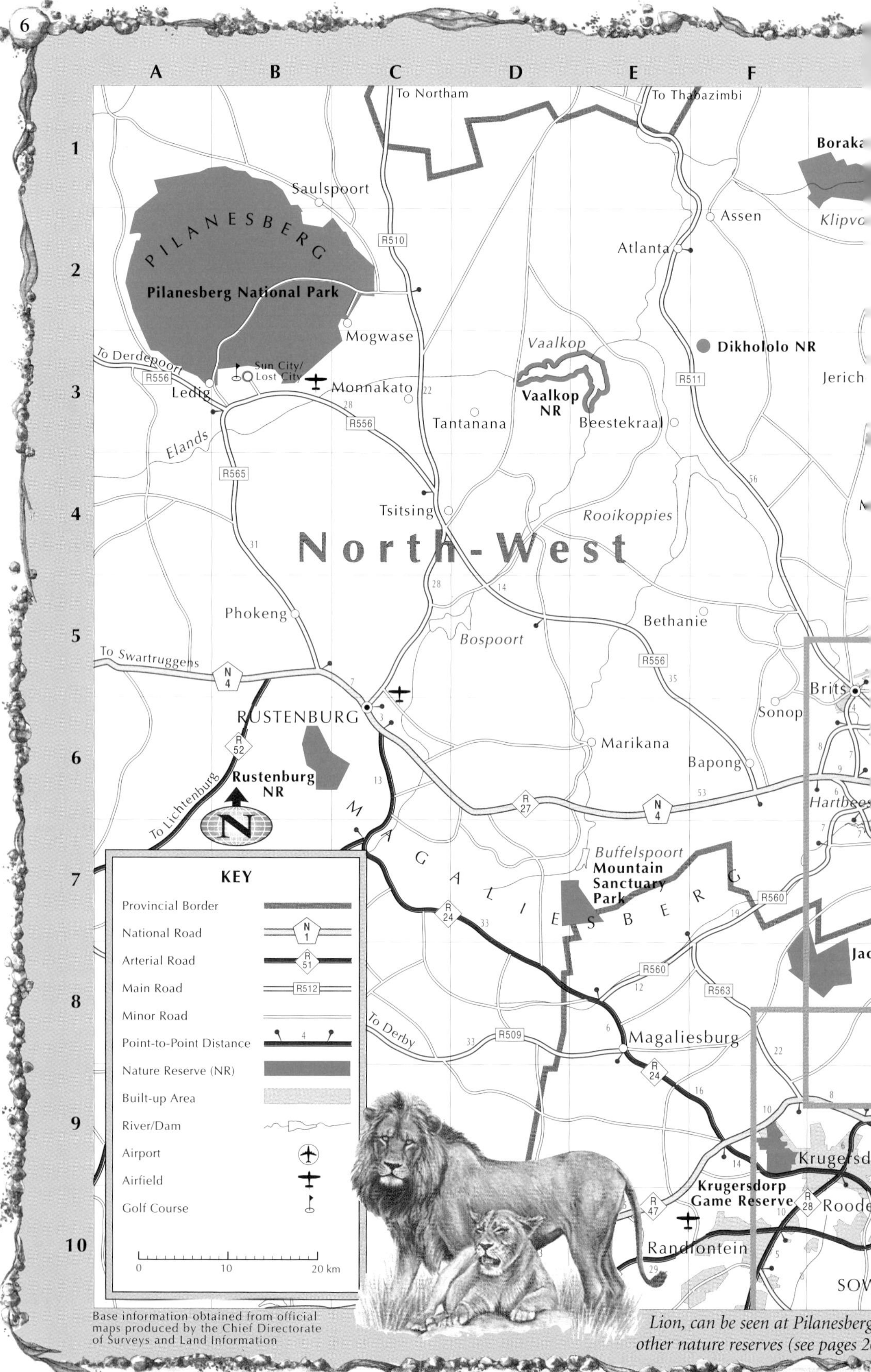

Base information obtained from official maps produced by the Chief Directorate of Surveys and Land Information

Lion, can be seen at Pilanesberg other nature reserves (see pages 26

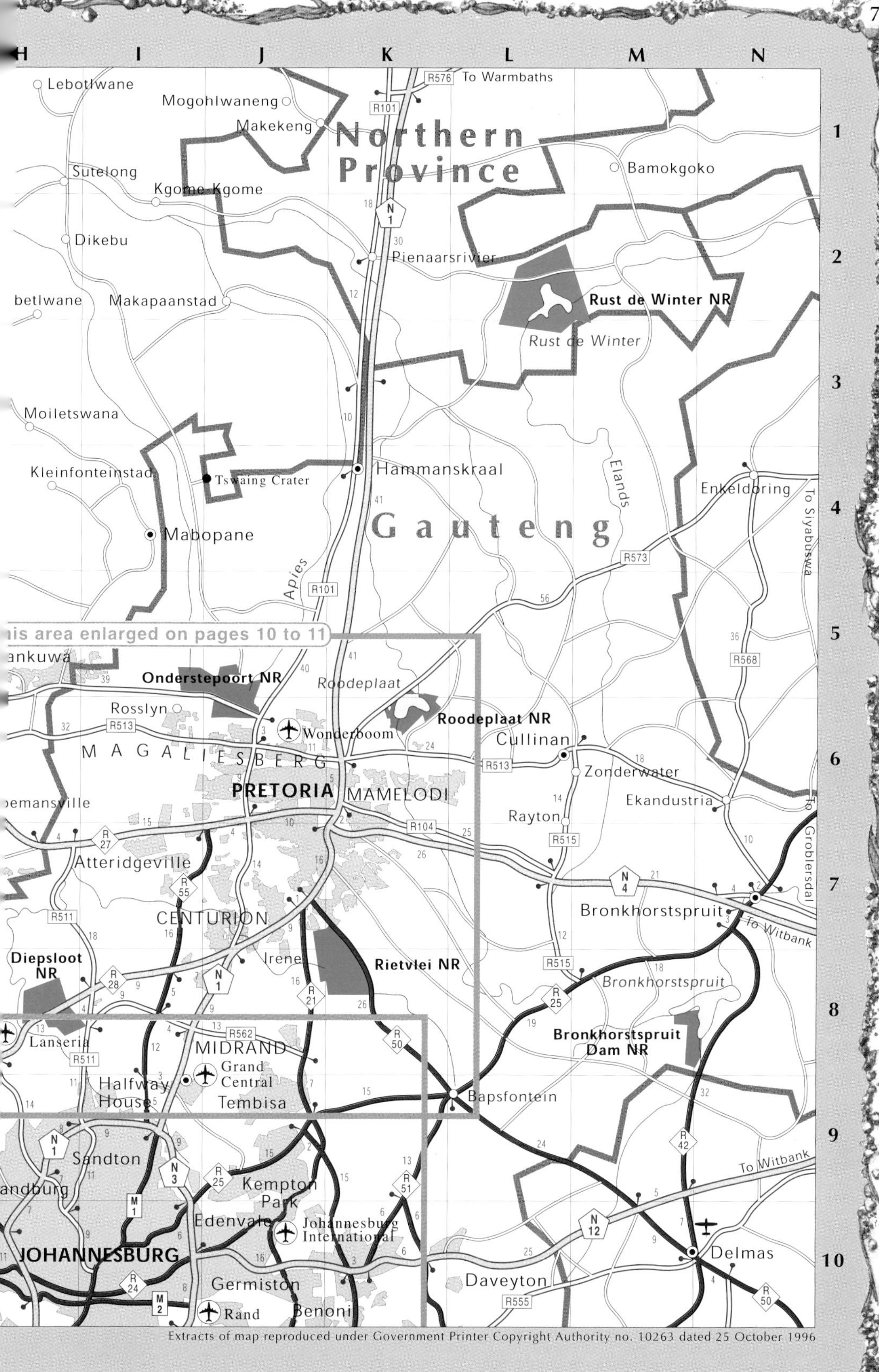

Extracts of map reproduced under Government Printer Copyright Authority no. 10263 dated 25 October 1996

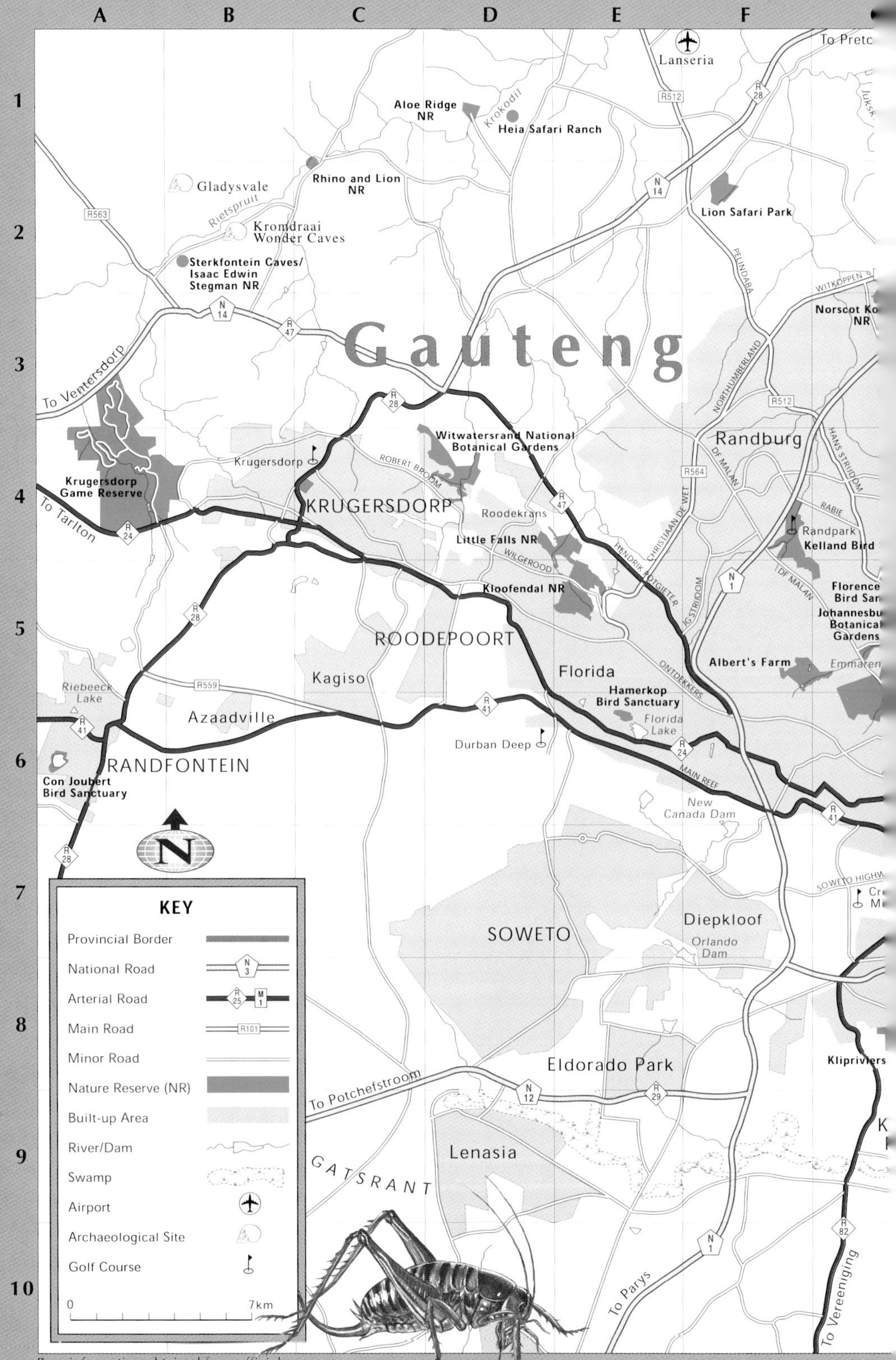

A B C D E F

Lanseria
R512
R28
To Pretoria
Aloe Ridge NR
Krokodil
Heia Safari Ranch
Gladysvale
Rhino and Lion NR
N14
Lion Safari Park
R563
Rietspruit
Kromdraai Wonder Caves
Sterkfontein Caves/ Isaac Edwin Stegman NR
Pelindaba
Witkoppen
Norscot Koppies NR
N14
R47
Gauteng
To Ventersdorp
Northumberland
R512
R28
Witwatersrand National Botanical Gardens
Randburg
Hans Strijdom
Krugersdorp
Robert Broom
R564
DF Malan
Christiaan de Wet
Krugersdorp Game Reserve
To Tarlton
R24
KRUGERSDORP
Roodekrans
R47
Rabie
Randpark
Kelland Bird
Little Falls NR
Wilgerood
Hendrik Potgieter
Kloofendal NR
N1
DF Malan
Strijdom
Florence Bird Sanctuary
Johannesburg Botanical Gardens
R28
ROODEPOORT
Albert's Farm
Emmarentia
Kagiso
Florida
Ontdekkers
Riebeeck Lake
R559
Hamerkop Bird Sanctuary
R41
Azaadville
R41
Florida Lake
Durban Deep
R24
RANDFONTEIN
Con Joubert Bird Sanctuary
Main Reef
New Canada Dam
R41
R28
Soweto Highway
SOWETO
Diepkloof
Orlando Dam
Eldorado Park
Klipriviersberg
To Potchefstroom
N12
R29
Lenasia
Gatsrant
R82
N1
To Parys
To Vereeniging

KEY

Provincial Border	
National Road	N3
Arterial Road	R25 M1
Main Road	R101
Minor Road	
Nature Reserve (NR)	
Built-up Area	
River/Dam	
Swamp	
Airport	
Archaeological Site	
Golf Course	

0 7km

Base information obtained from official maps produced by the Chief Directorate of Surveys and Land Information

King Cricket, a phenomenon of the city! (see page 69)

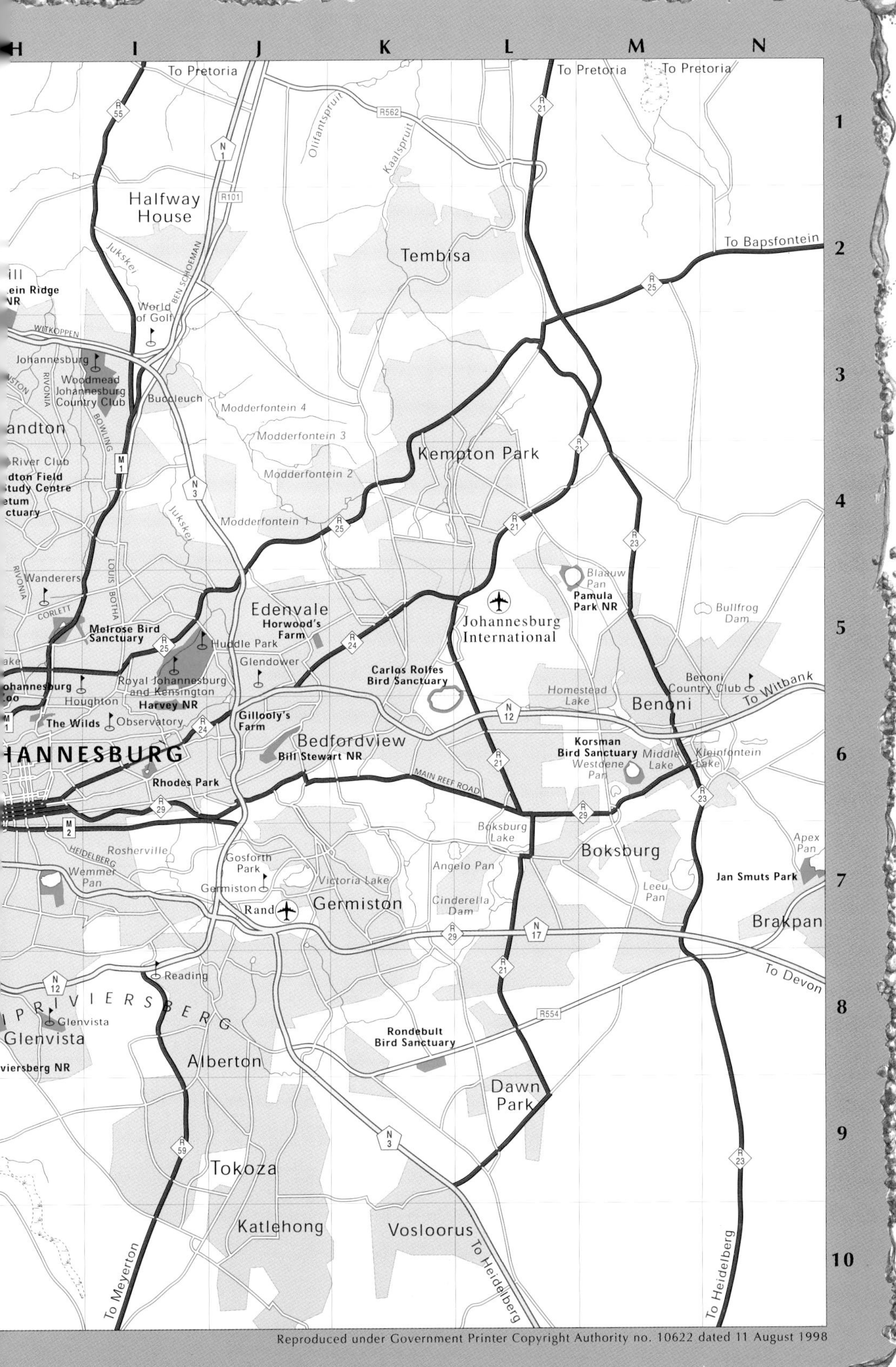

Reproduced under Government Printer Copyright Authority no. 10622 dated 11 August 1998

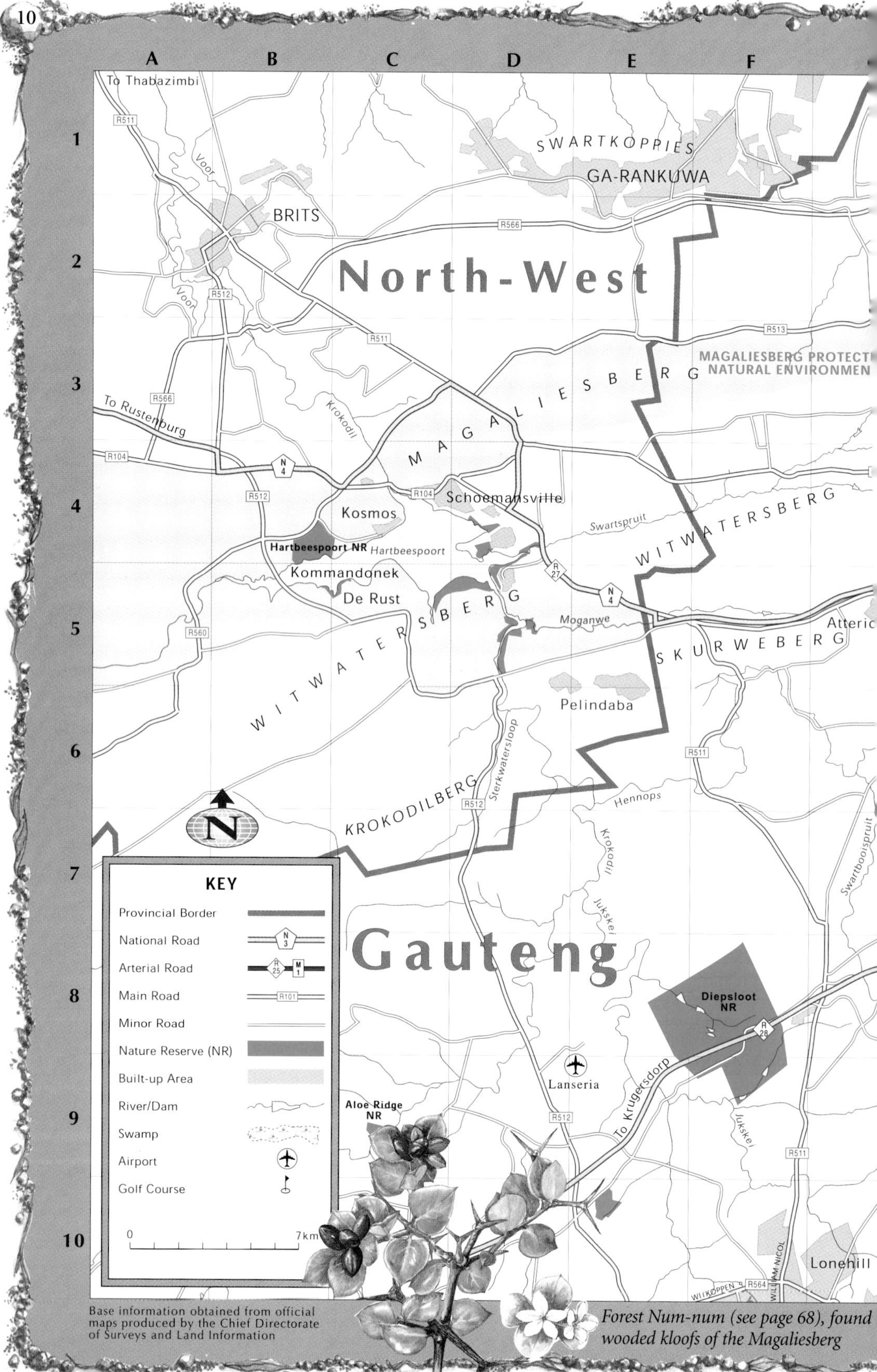

Base information obtained from official maps produced by the Chief Directorate of Surveys and Land Information

Forest Num-num (see page 68), found i wooded kloofs of the Magaliesberg

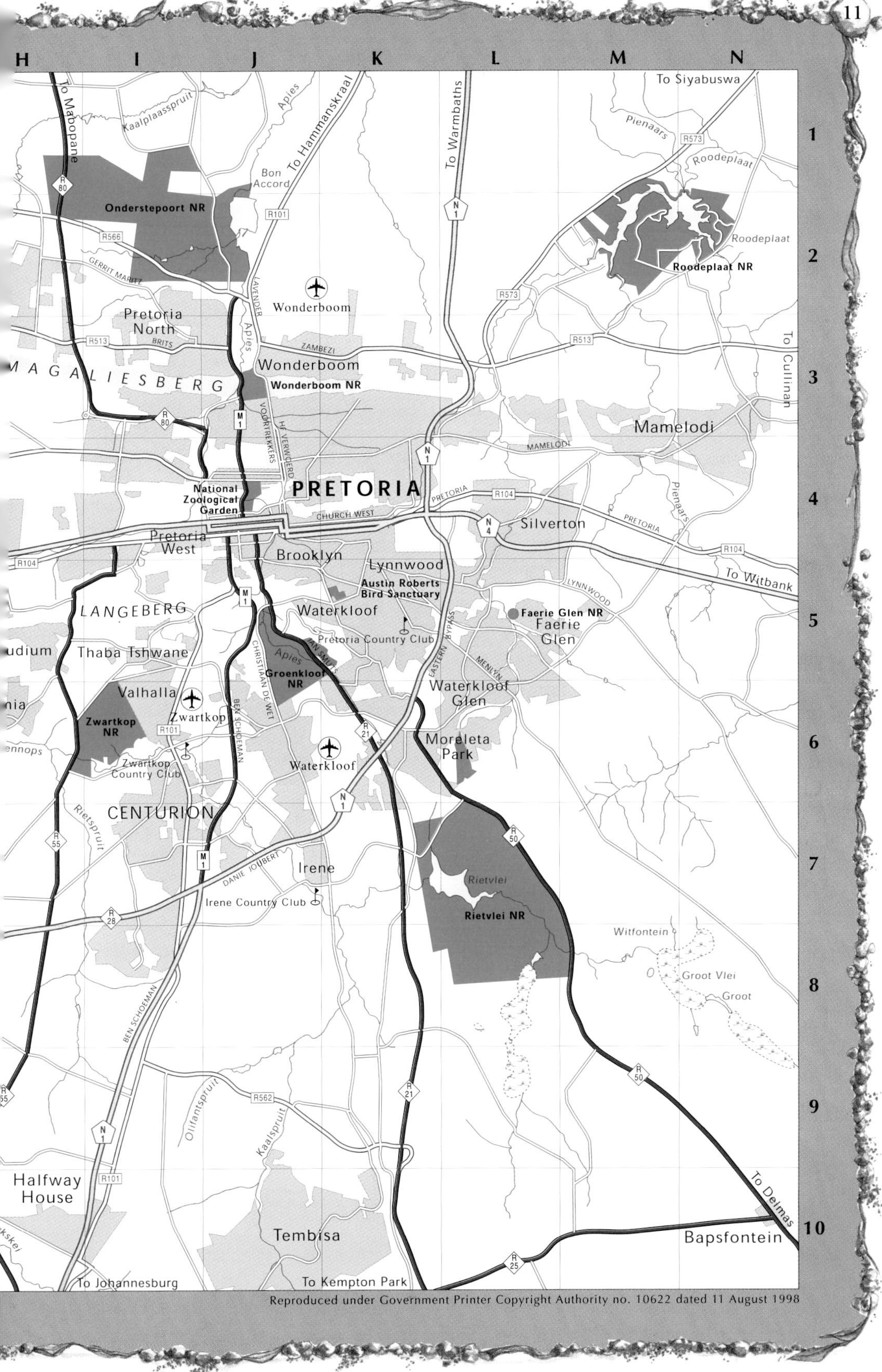

Reproduced under Government Printer Copyright Authority no. 10622 dated 11 August 1998

Places to Visit and Things to Do

Many people will tell you that Johannesburg and its surrounding areas have little to offer the eco-tourist. Nothing could be further from the truth. Use the colour-coded grids on the following pages along with their corresponding maps on pages 4 - 11 to Discover the Magic of Gauteng.

Key to Map Colours

Map 1 (see pages 4-5)

Map 2 (see pages 6-7)

Map 3 (see pages 8-9)

Map 4 (see pages 10-11)

Key to Authorities

MUN Municipal

NBI National Botanical Institute

NFI Northern Flagship Institution

NWPB North West Parks Board

PROV Provincial

PVT Private

Contents

- Abseiling 20
- Air Adventure 20
- Air Flips 20
- Annual Cultural Festivals 20
- Astronomy / Star-gazing 21
- Birding 15
- Botanical Gardens 25
- Bungee Jumping 20
- Canoeing / Kayaking 19
- Curios / Street Trading 21
- Dams and Smaller Lakes 25
- Eco-tourist Accommodation 16
- Emergency Numbers 13
- Fishing 16
- Flea Markets 21
- Foreign Exchange 13
- Game Parks / Reserves 27
- Game Viewing 14
- Golf Courses and Theme Parks 18
- Hiking 17
- Historical Sites and Monuments 23
- Horse and Pony Riding / Horse Performances 16
- Horse Racing 19
- Indigenous Vegetation 14
- Information Centres and Services 12
- Meanders and Rambles 20
- Mountain Biking 16
- Museums 24
- Natural History Sites 22
- Nature Reserves 26, 27
- Night Activities 21
- Parks 27
- River Rafting 19
- Rock Climbing 20
- Scenic Train Trips 13
- Tour Companies 13
- Transport and Travel 13
- Vehicle Hire 13
- Watersports 19
- Yachting 19
- Zoological Gardens / Captive Animals 25

Information Centres and Services

CONTACT	*TEL NO.*
Benoni Publicity Association	(011) 422-3
Bird Watching	N/L
Boksburg Publicity Association	(011) 917-1
Botanical Society	(011) 482-1
British Airways Travel Clinic	(011) 807-3
Department of Home Affairs (Visa Section)	(011) 836-3
Eastern Gauteng Tourism	N/L
Gauteng Tourism	(011) 340-9
Hartbeespoort Publicity	(012) 253-0
Info Africa - Pretoria	(012) 660-0
Johannesburg Hiking Association	(011) 465-9
Tourism - Johannesburg	(011) 784-1
National Parks Board	(012) 343-97
North West Parks Board Tourist Information	(014) 556-29
Pilanesberg National Park	(014) 555-53
Pretoria Tourism Info Bureau	(012) 308-89
Rand Piscatorial Association (Angling)	(011) 837-27
Roodepoort Publicity Association	(011) 672-95
Satour (S.A. Tourism Board)	(012) 482-62 (011) 970-16
Sun City Publicity	(014) 557-10
Sun International Central Reservations (www.sun-international.com)	(011) 780-78

Municipal Sub-structure

Johannesburg:	
Eastern MSS	(011) 881-64
Northern MSS	(011) 686-26
Southern MSS	(011) 407-63
Western MSS	(011) 672-95
Pretoria:	
Pretoria Metropolitan Substructure	(012) 308-791

ICLE HIRE

TACT	TEL NO.
	0800 02 1111
t	0800 01 6622
on Wheels (motorhome rental)	(011) 475 1653
	0800 600 136
ial	0800 13 1000 (after hours 0800 11 8898)
mobiles (4x4 rentals)	(011) 805-4017

Please note that telephone numbers do change. For further information or clarification consult the local telephone directories, or contact 1023 for directory assistance. The publishers welcome feedback from users of these pages. N/L = Not Listed.

EMERGENCY NUMBERS

CONTACT	TEL NO.
Ambulance	999
Automatic Phone Weather Service	082 2311659
Automobile Association of South Africa	080001 0101
Crime Stop Emergencies	(011) 435-3805
Directory Enquiries	1023
Metro Rail Train Emergency	0801 11 01 41
S.A. Police Flying Squad	10111

NSPORT AND TRAVEL

ITACT	TEL NO.
Train (luxury cross-country rail service)	(011) 773-7631
Council Bus Services Pretoria	(012) 308-0839
ıound Coach Lines (reservations)	(011) 830-1301
Taxi	(011) 648-1212
o Rail Passenger Services	(011) 773-5878
opolitan Johannesburg Bus Services	(011) 403-4300
slux	(011) 774-3333

FOREIGN EXCHANGE

CONTACT	TEL NO.
American Express	(011) 880-8382
Rennies	080011 1177
Thomas Cook	(011) 444-8040

NIC TRAIN TRIPS

ITACT	TEL NO.	NOTES
ersdorp Steam Railway	(011) 888-1154	Short trips on old steam train; great for kids.
aliesberg Express	(011) 888-1154	Regular diesel train excursions into the Magaliesberg.

Leopard Tortoise
(see page 49)

JR COMPANIES

TACT	TEL NO.	NOTES
tu Tours	N/L	Day and overnight tours to Soweto; jazz tours also available.
Adventures	086 0000 111	Youth Student Travel Specialist. Variety of tour packages from bungee jumping to desert treks.
an Adventures	(011) 660-3542	Variety of packages including mountain biking, river rafting/canoeing, and microlighting.
an Impressions	(011) 609-5867	Quality camping safaris and cycling tours.
ela Africa	083 659 9928	Day and away tours.
Access	(011) 477-3676	Making the natural environment accessible to disabled people.
to Face Tours	(011) 331-6109	Extensive tours of Soweto.
Reef Guides	(011) 496-1400	Information, training and guided tours of Johannesburg.
a Bus	(011) 914-4321	Excursions and tours.
zo Tours	(011) 838-2667	Soweto, Johannesburg, Gold Reef City and beyond.
ıa Country Homes and Trails	(012) 346-3550/1/2	Affordable activity holiday getaways.
ndraai Conservancy	(011) 957-0034	Variety of trails, tours, caves, horse trails and fossil sites.
aliesberg Information, rs and Reservations	(014) 577-1733	Information about guided tours and outdoor activities in this area.
erness Wheels Africa	(011) 648-5737	Wheelchair safari exploration.
ah Tours	(011) 781-2093	Day trips from Johannesburg.
zi Tours	N/L	Tours to Sharpeville, Boipatong and Orange Farm.

Game Viewing

CONTACT OR VISIT	TEL NO.	MAP REF	NOTES
Big Five			
Pilanesberg National Park	(014) 555-5351	B2	Home of the Big 5; next to Sun City.
Heia Safari Ranch	(011) 659-0605	D1	Well stocked reserve including rhino and buffalo.
Smaller Game			
Abe Bailey Nature Reserve	(018) 786-3431	C4	Springbok, wildebeest, hartebeest.
Suikerbosrand Nature Reserve	(011) 904-3933	J6	Varied wildlife.
Dikhololo Nature Reserve	(012) 277-1200	F3	Small antelope; game drives.
Borakololo Nature Reserve	N/L	G1	Abundance of smaller game; huge flocks of waterfowl.
Rustenburg Nature Reserve	(014) 533-2050	B6	Kudu, Red Hartebeest, springbok, sable, roan.
Klipriviersberg Nature Reserve	(011) 680-4153	G8	Small mammals.
Krugersdorp Game Reserve	(011) 665-4342	A4	Lion, giraffe, zebra, rhino.
Lion Safari Park	(011) 460-1814	F2	More than 50 lions.
Rhino and Lion Nature Reserve	(011) 957-0109	C2	White Rhino, lion.
De Wildt Cheetah Centre	(012) 504-1921	G2	Guided tours give insight into breeding programmes and wildlife conservation.
Groenkloof Nature Reserve	(012) 440-8316	J5	Blesbok, zebra, impala, kudu, wildebeest.
Rietvlei Nature Reserve	(012) 345-2274	L7	Oribi, White Rhino, Black Wildebeest.

Cross- berry Raisin
(see page 58)

Black Rhinocero
(see page 87)

Indigenous Vegetation

Read Sappi Tree Spotting Highveld for detailed information.

CONTACT OR VISIT	TEL NO.	MAP REF	TREE LIST AVAILABLE	NOTES
Springs Pioneer Park	N/L	L4		Lovely gardens with aloes.
Suikerbosrand Nature Reserve	(011) 904-3933	J6	•	743 plant species; varied terrain.
Vaal Dam Nature Reserve	(016) 371-1391	K9		Riverine vegetation.
Mountain Sanctuary Park Nature Reserve	(014) 534-0114	E7	•	Protea plantations.
Rustenburg Nature Reserve	(014) 533-2050	B6	•	Typical bushveld vegetation.
Vaalkop Dam Nature Reserve	(014) 555-5351	D3		Thornveld, savannah, riverine.
Klipriviersberg Nature Reserve	(011) 680-4153	G8	•	Varied indigenous vegetation.
Kloofendal Nature Reserve	(011) 679-5912	E5	•	Walks; indigenous trees.
Norscot Koppies Nature Reserve	(011) 465-2239	G3	•	Small reserve with a variety of indigenous tr
Plant Park	(011) 463-5773	G3	•	Garden centre; tea garden and children's play
The Wilds	N/L	H6		Abundant indigenous vegetation.
Witwatersrand National Botanical Gardens	(011) 958-1750	D4	•	Landscaped and natural veld; beautiful water
Diepsloot Nature Reserve	(011) 464-1510	F8	•	Lovely savannah and bushveld vegetation.
Faerie Glen Nature Reserve	(012) 348-1265	L5	•	Variety of indigenous trees.
Groenkloof Nature Reserve	(012) 448316/ 447131	J5	•	Sweet Thorn, Broad-pod SplendidAcacias.
Hartbeespoort Dam Nature Reserve (Oberon)	(012) 244-1353	B4	•	Cussonia, Rock Karee-rhus and Stinkwood, among may others.
National Botanical Gardens	(012) 804-3200	L4	•	Lovely landscaped gardens; picnic concerts or alternate Sundays in winter.
Rietvlei Nature Reserve	(012) 345-2274	L7	•	Open grassveld with White Stinkwood, Acacias, 21 indigenous tree species.
Vergenoeg Nature Reserve	(012) 207-1007	B4	•	Wide variety of indigenous trees and flowers.
Wonderboom Nature Reserve	(012) 543-0918	J3	•	1000-year-old giant fig tree.
Zwartkop Nature Reserve	N/L	I6	•	Typical bushveld vegetation.

ING

›A (011) 789-1122

ACT OR VISIT	TEL NO.	MAP REF	NOTES
iley Nature Reserve	(018) 786-3431	C4	400 ha vleis; fish eagles, flamingos, painted snipe; Goliath Heron, Shell Duck; birders paradise.
spruit Environmental Centre	(011) 360-2203/4	L4	One of the 12 Ramsar Wetland sites in South Africa
ale Bird Sanctuary	N/L	L5	300 species; 1 000 ha on Blesbokspruit.
Thru	(056) 816-2200	J9	Variety of water and bush birds, 180 bird species.
osrand Nature Reserve	(011) 904-3933	J6	Over 200 species.
am Nature Reserve	(016) 371-1391	K9	Variety of water fowl.
lolo Nature Reserve	(011) 465-5423	G1	300 bird species; birdwatcher's paradise.
orstspruit Dam Nature Reserve	N/L	G1	Impressive variety of birds; waterfowl.
ain Sanctuary Park Nature Reserve	(014) 534-0114	E7	Abundant birdlife.
Winter Nature Reserve	N/L	L2	360 species.
p Dam	(014) 555-5351	D3	Many species; bird sanctuary
idge Nature Reserve	(011) 957-2070	D1	Excellent birdwatching area.
Rolfes Bird Sanctuary	N/L	K5	90 ha; Grey-headed Gulls breed in winter; breeding ground for waders.
ubert Bird Sanctuary	N/L	A6	150 species including flamingos; excellent viewing hide; permanent pan.
Park	(011) 888-4831	G5	Bird sanctuary; viewing hides.
ce Bloom Bird Sanctuary	N/L	G5	Viewing hides; major environmental education centre.
kop Bird Sanctuary	N/L	E6	Bushveld and waterbird reserve; 1 837 ha; large dam.
d Bird Sanctuary	N/L	G4	Spotted Eagle Owls, weavers, bishops.
viersberg Nature Reserve	(011) 680-4153	G8	120 bird species.
ndal Nature Reserve	(011) 679-5912	E5	Diverse bird population.
an's Bird Sanctuary	N/L	M6	163 species including ibis and flamingos; 50 ha; breeding sanctuary; viewing through fence.
se Wild Bird Sanctuary	N/L	I5	Wading birds; dam; reedswamps; veld.
a Park Nature Reserve	N/L	L5	Variety of waterbirds.
ebult Bird Sanctuary	N/L	K8	195 species; exceptional water birds; 94 ha; marshlands; reedbeds; islands; 8 viewing hides.
atersrand National Botanical Gardens	(011) 958-1750	D4	230 species.
Roberts Bird Sanctuary	(012) 44-8316	K5	Large numbers of heron and egret. Benches around perimeter; 11 ha; dam; viewing hide.
loot Nature Reserve	(011) 464-1510	F8	1 000's of species; only open to bird clubs by arrangement.
Glen Nature Reserve	(012) 348-1265	L5	Large variety of birdlife.
kloof Nature Reserve	(012) 440-8316	J5	Varied birdlife
ops Hiking Trail (Hartbeespoort Dam)	(012) 253-0266	D4	Abundant birdlife.
liesberg Protected Natural Environment	N/L	A-K 3-5	Cape Vulture and other species can be seen throughout this area.
lei Nature Reserve	(012) 345-2274	L7	240 species.
eplaat Nature Reserve	N/L	M2	75 species.
n Buildings	(012) 319-1500	L4	Prolific birdlife; beautiful walks.
noeg Nature Reserve	(012) 207-1007	B4	Large Cape Vulture colony.

** Please note that telephone numbers do change. further information or clarification consult the local phone directories, or contact 1023 for directory stance. The publishers welcome feedback from users nese pages. N/L = Not Listed.*

Black Eagle
(see page 75)

Fish Eagle
(see page 83)

Eco-Tourist Accommodation

CONTACT OR VISIT	TEL NO.	MAP REF	NOTES
Mount Grace Hotel	(014) 577-1350	E8	Beautiful hotel set in Magaliesberg foothills.
Valley Lodge Hotel	(014) 577-1301	E8	Perfect for Sunday lunch or weekend getaway.
Aloe Ridge Hotel	(011) 957-2070	D1	Beautiful hotel hideaway; excellent meals and accommodatior
Heia Safari Ranch	(011) 659-0605	D1	Lovely hotel with small game reserve and Zulu village.
Amanzingwe	(012) 205-1108	D6	Bushveld lodge; small game; bushwalks; fully equipped.

Horse and Pony Riding / Horse Performances

CONTACT OR VISIT	TEL NO.	MAP REF	NOTES
Roberts Farm Horse Trails	(014) 577-3332	C7	Trails through Magaliesberg mountains.
Broadacres	(011) 705-2127	G2	Riding lessons and out-rides available.
Lipizzaner Centre	(011) 702-2103	H2	Performances by the Lipizzaner stallions.
Jacana Trails	(012) 346-3550/1/2	K5	Choice trails on private farms.
Paddle Power Horse Trails	(011) 794-3098	H10	Half-day rides along Jukskei River.
Rietvlei Nature Reserve	(012) 345-2274	L7	Beautiful trail rides.

Fishing

CONTACT OR VISIT	TEL NO.	MAP REF	NOTES
Smilin Thru	(056) 816-2200	J9	Fishing on the banks of the Vaal River.
Vaal Dam Nature Reserve	(016) 371-1391	J9	Barbel, carp, yellowfish among other varieties.
Vaalkop Dam	(014) 555-5351	D3	Variety of freshwater fish can be caught.
Aloe Ridge Game Reserve	(011) 975-2070	D1	Trout fishing
Footloose Trout Farm	(011) 464-2201/2	G2	For fly fisherman and amateurs; dams stocked with trout, barbel and bass; pub and children's play area.
Kromdraai Conservancy Trails	(011) 957-0106	B2	Rainbow Trout farm.
Rietvlei Nature Reserve	(012) 345-2274	L7	Fishing on the Rietvlei dam; open 7 days a week.
Roodeplaat Dam Nature Reserve	N/L	M2	Popular angling venue.

Fishing tackle

Mountain Biking

CONTACT OR VISIT	TEL NO.	MAP REF	NOTES
Roberts Farm Horse Trails	(014) 577-3332	C7	Mountain biking trails through the Magaliesberg mountains.
Johannesburg Mountain Bicycle Club	N/L	H4	Weekly meetings and rides for enthusiasts.
Pretoria Mountain Bicycle Club	N/L	K3	Weekend rides in and around Pretoria.
GroenKloof Nature Reserve	(012) 440-8316	J3	Entrance at Fountains Valley

NG

-Iikingway Board www.wildnetafrica.com/travelsa/jacana
ɔurg Hiking Association (011) 465-9888

ACT OR VISIT	TEL NO.	MAP REF	NOTES
Thru	(056) 816-2200	J9	Three excellent trails of 3 km, 6 km and 20 km.
›osrand Nature Reserve	(011) 904-3933	J6	Network of trails; 1-6 days; overnight camps.
Rivers Nature Trail	N/L	H7	12,5 km along Klip, Vaal and Suikerbosrand rivers.
lolo Nature Reserve	N/L	G1	Self-guided walks.
ain Sanctuary Park Nature Reserve	(014) 534-0114	E7	Day walks; beautiful rock pools.
s Farm Horse Trails	(014) 577-3332	C7	Hiking in Magaliesberg mountains.
Winter Nature Reserve	N/L	L2	Close to Pretoria; popular picnic and braai venue.
burg Nature Reserve	(014) 533-2050	B6	Various day hikes through beautiful kloofs and bushveld vegetation.
p Nature Reserve	(014) 555-5351	D3	Day hikes; small dam; overnight accommodation.
idge Game Reserve	(011) 957 2070	D1	Hiking trails along river.
ly's Farm	(011) 453-8066	J6	10-15 km walks; nice views.
Nature Reserve	N/L	I6	Day hikes including Dassie Trail.
Edwin Stegman Nature Reserve	(011) 956-6342	B2	Home of the Sterkfontein Caves.
viersberg Nature Reserve	(011) 680-4153	G8	Site of remains of Iron Age villages.
ndal Nature Reserve	(011) 679-5912	E5	Walking trails; old gold-mine shafts.
draai Conservancy Trails	(011) 957-0034	B2	Day and overnight trails; 5-11 km; caves.
ot Koppies Nature Reserve	(011) 465-2230	G3	One open day per month; ancient rock formations.
ntein Ridge Nature Reserve	N/L	H2	25 ha; just north of Sandton; short walks.
Glen Nature Reserve	(012) 348-1265	L5	Day hikes; 14 km.
kloof Nature Reserve	(012) 440-8316	J5	Hiking trails, 10 ½ and 4 ½ kms.
eespoort Dam Nature Reserve	(012) 253-0266	B4	This reserve borders the popular Hartbeespoort Dam.
ops Hiking Trail	(012) 253-0266	D5	Hartbeespoort Dam, 2-day trails; base camps; swimming holes.
ops Picnic Spots	(012) 253-0266	D5	Various trails, 6 - 11 km.
liesberg Protected Natural onment	N/L	A-K 3-5	Wide variety of hiking trails throughout this area.
leta Spruit Trail	N/L	K6	10 km day hike.
lei Nature Reserve	(012) 345-2274	L7	Day hikes; well-established trails, overnight hikes
noeg Nature Reserve	(012) 207-1007	B4	Variety of short hikes and walks.
derboom Nature Reserve	(012) 543-0918	J3	Day walks; caves; ancient rock formations.
tkop Nature Reserve	N/L	I6	Small reserve; manageable trails.

Dassie (see page 92)

annesburg and surrounding areas offer wonderful hiking opportunities.

Please note that telephone numbers do change. For further information or clarification consult the local telephone directories, or contact 1023 for directory assistance. The publishers welcome feedback from users of these pages. N/L = Not Listed.

Damselfly (see page 57)

Golf courses in and around Johannesburg are among the best in the c

Golf Courses and Theme Parks

AUTH = Authority

CONTACT OR VISIT	TEL NO.	MAP REF	AUTH	NOTES
Emfuleni Country Club	(016) 932-1162	G8	Pvt	18 holes; pro shop; Tuesday-Sunday.
Heidelberg Golf Course	(016) 349-1061	K6	Pvt	9 holes; pro shop; Monday-Sunday.
Vereeniging Country Club	(016) 422-0036	H7	Pvt	18 holes; pro shop; open 7 days a week.
Lost City Golf Course	(014) 557-3000	B3	Pvt	18 holes; pro shop; open 7 days a week.
Sun City Golf Course	(014) 557-1000	B3	Pvt	18 holes; pro shop; open 7 days a week.
Alberton Golf Course / Reading Country Club	(011) 907-8906	I8	Pvt	18 holes; pro shop; Tuesday-Sunday; Saturday pm and Sunday am - members only, with guests.
Benoni Country Club	(011) 849-5211	N5	Pvt	18 holes; pro shop; Tuesday-Sunday; Saturday - members o
Crown Mines Golf Club	(011) 496-1505	G7	Pvt	18 holes; pro shop; Tuesday-Sunday; Saturday am - member
Durban Deep Golf Course	(011) 763-5892	D6	Pvt	18 holes; pro shop; Tuesday-Sunday; Thursday am - pensione Saturday - competitions.
Germiston Golf Club	(011) 827-8950	J7	Pvt	18 holes; pro shop; Tuesday-Sunday; Saturday & Sunday am members only.
Glendower Golf Course	(011) 453-1013	J5	Pvt	18 holes; pro shop; Tuesday-Sunday; Saturday pm and Sunday am - members only.
Glenvista Country Club	(011) 432-3150	H8	Pvt	18 holes; pro shop; Tuesday-Sunday; Saturday - members or
Houghton Golf Club	(011) 728-7337	I5	Pvt	18 holes; pro shop; Tuesday-Sunday; Thursday, Saturday, Sunday mornings - members only.
Huddle Park Golf Course	(011) 640-2748	J5	Pvt	3 x 18 holes; open 7 days a week.
Krugersdorp Golf Course	(011) 660-4365	C4	Pvt	18 holes; Tuesday-Sunday; Saturday - members only.
Observatory Golf Club	(011) 648-9579	I6	Mun	18 holes; pro shop; Tuesday-Sunday; Saturday - members on
Rand Park Golf Club	(011) 676-1691	F4	Pvt	2 x 18 holes; pro shop; Tuesday-Sunday; Saturday - members
River Club Golf Course	(011) 783-1166	H4	Pvt	18 holes; golf shop; Tuesday-Sunday.
Roodepoort Country Club	(011) 958-1905	E5	Pvt	18 holes; Tuesday-Sunday.
Royal Johannesburg and Kensington Golf Club	(011) 640-3021	I5	Pvt	18 holes; pro shop; Tuesday-Sunday; Saturday and Sunday - members only.
Wanderers Golf Club	(011) 447-3311	H5	Pvt	18 holes; pro shop; Saturday and Sunday mornings - members only.
Woodmead Johannesburg Country Club	(011) 803-3018	I3	Pvt	36 holes; open 7 days a week; visitors must be with a member
World of Golf	(011) 802-5864	I3	Pvt	35 acre, world class golfing theme park; bunkers, chipping, pu driving; 12 different target bent grass greens; world class dem centre; open 7 days a week.
Irene Country Club	(012) 667-1081	J7	Pvt	18 holes; pro shop; open 7 days a week.
Pretoria Country Club	(012) 460-6241	K5	Pvt	18 holes; pro shop; open Tuesday-Sunday for members only a other Gauteng Golf/Country Club Card holders. Tennis, squas and bowling facilities.
Zwartkop Country Club	(012) 654-1144	I6	Pvt	18 holes; pro shop; Monday- Sunday; Saturday - members on

HORSE RACING

For general information: (011) 400-1222

CONTACT OR VISIT	TEL NO.	MAP REF	NOTES
Gosforth Park	(011) 873-1000	J7	Popular racecourse on the East Rand.
Turffontein	(011) 681-1500	H7	Johannesburg's oldest racecourse.

·ITING

·ACT OR VISIT	TEL NO.	MAP REF	NOTES
horstspruit Dam	N/L	M1	Suitable for smaller sailing boats.
·am Nature Reserve	N/L	K9	The Vaal Dam is a popular yachting venue.
·le Winter Nature Reserve	N/L	L2	Sailing on dam.
rella Dam	N/L	L7	Home of the East Rand Yacht Club.
arentia Dam	(011) 646-5309	G5	Sailing and canoeing; no powerboats.

Sail sheets

WATERSPORTS

CONTACT OR VISIT	TEL NO.	MAP REF	NOTES
Bronkhorstspruit Dam Nature Reserve	N/L	M1	Popular over weekends.
Vaal Dam Nature Reserve	N/L	K9	All varieties of watersports and boating activities.
Buffelspoort Dam	(014)572-3174	E7	Power boating and waterskiing.
Rust de Winter Nature Reserve	N/L	L2	Popular waterskiing venue.
Boksburg Lake	(011) 899-4499	L7	Central venue on East Rand for watersports.
Middle Lake	N/L	M6	Benoni's main lake; smaller boats preferable.
Bon Accord Dam	N/L	K2	Popular watersports venue; 10 minutes from Pretoria.
Hartbeespoort Dam	(012) 253-0266	C4	Attracts many watersport enthusiasts.
Roodeplaat Dam Nature Reserve	N/L	M2	Launch sites for power boats.

·NOEING/KAYAKING

·ther information phone Canoe and Kayak World (011) 475-8156

·TACT OR VISIT	TEL NO.	MAP REF	NOTES
River	N/L	H8	Great for weekend or day excursions.
·niston Lake	N/L	J7	Popular for training and short canoeing sessions.
·le Power Rivertrips	(011) 794-3098	C4	Guided river adventures.
·deplaat Dam Nature ·rve	N/L	M2	Olympic standard canoeing/rowing course.

Red-knobbed Coot
(see page 83)

Please note that telephone ·nbers do change. For further ·ormation or clarification ·sult the local telephone ·ectories, or contact 1023 for ·ectory assistance. The ·blishers welcome feedback ·n users of these pages. ·L = Not Listed.

RIVER RAFTING

CONTACT OR VISIT	TEL NO.	MAP REF	NOTES
River Adventures	(056) 803-9775	F8	Offers rafting on the Vaal River; not suitable for children under 10.
River Tours and Safaris	(011) 803-9775	H7	Paddling on the Vaal River; spectacular scenery.
Smilin Thru	(056) 816-2200	E8	River rafting on the Vaal River
Vaal River	N/L	H8	Popular rafting area.
Paddle Power Adventures	(011) 794-3098	C4	Guided adventures down various Highveld rivers including the Crocodile River.

Yellow-billed Ducks
(see page 82)

Black Eagle
(see page 75)

Air Flips

CONTACT	TEL NO.	NOTES
Executive Aerospace	0800 312177	Twin-engine charters around South Africa.
Court Helicopters	(011) 827-8907	Helicopter flights in and around Johannesburg.
Air Champagne	(011) 788-8957	30-minute flights over Johannesburg by day or night, meal included.

Air Adventure

CONTACT	TEL NO.	NOTES
Paragliding Afrika	(011) 880-9229	Weekend courses in paragliding and paramotor, kite carting, kite surfing.
Airtrack Adventures (Ballooning)	(011) 957-2322	Sunrise balloon trips over Crocodile River Valley.

Cape Dwarf Gecko
(see page 48)

Bungee Jumping/Rock Climbing/Abseiling

CONTACT OR VISIT	TEL NO.	MAP REF	NOTES
SA Bungee CC	(011) 805-4565	–	Various locations in and around Johannesburg.
SA Climb Inn	083 737 8091	J5	Indoor climbing gym.
Fernkloof	(014) 537-2363	E4	Abseiling and rock climbing in magnificent gorge in Magaliesberg mountains.
Magaliesberg Protected Natural Environment	N/L	A-K 3-5	Wide variety of mountain and kloof climbs in this area.
Mountain Club of South Africa	(011) 807-1310	A-K 3-4	Private club. Issues permits for various climbs in Magaliesberg.

Meanders and Rambles

CONTACT OR VISIT	TEL NO.	MAP REF	NOTES
Magalies Meander	(014) 577-1845	E-G 6-8	1 hr from Johannesburg; day out for the family; restaurants, hotels, hiking and shopping.
Crocodile Ramble	(011) 662-2810 www.crocodileramble.co.za	G7-9	Arts, crafts, adventure activities restaurants and accommodation.

Jazz singer Thandi Klassen performs at a cultural festival.

Annual Cultural Festivals

Computicket 083 9090909 Satour (011) 970-1669 (012) 347-0600

CONTACT OR VISIT	TEL NO.	MAP REF	NOTES
Arts Alive (September)	(011) 838-6407	H6	Johannesburg's annual festival of dance, drama and music.
Rand Easter Show (April) National Exhibition Centre	(011) 494-9111 (011) 679-4422	G7	Popular trade fair; activities for entire family.
Getaway Show	(011) 783-7030	F3	Africa's largest holiday, travel and ecotourism exhibition.
94.7 Highveld Stereo Outdoor Adventure show	(011) 803-9362	H2	Outdoor exhibitions, events and prizes
Pretoria International Show (September)	(012) 327-1487	J4	Pretoria's annual agricultural fair.

Flea Markets

VISIT	MAP REF	NOTES
Bruma Flea Market World	I6	Bruma Lake - daily.
Horwood's Farm	J5	Edenvale; Saturdays, Sundays and public holidays.
Michaelmount Market	H3	Bryanston - Thursday and Saturday.
Rosebank Rooftop Market	H5	Rosebank - Sundays and public holidays.
Killarney Rooftop	H6	Killarney - Sundays and public holidays.
Mai Mai Market	H6	End Street Johannesburg; daily.
Newtown Market (Market Theatre)	H6	Saturdays only.
Harbour Market	F4	Randburg Waterfront - daily.
Hatfield Market	K4	Hatfield Plaza - Sundays.
Irene Village Market	K7	2nd and last Saturday.

Wood carving of hippo

Curios/Street Trading

VISIT	MAP REF	NOTES
Cradock Avenue, Rosebank	H5	High quality crafts from all over Africa sold daily.
Diagonal Street (CBD)	H6	Mix of Indian and African traders, small shops full of odd and interesting curios; open daily.
Marcia Street, Bruma Lake	I6	Wide variety of African handicrafts; open daily.
Oriental Plaza, Jeppe Street, Fordsburg	H6	Famous Indian traders' market, open daily.
William Nicol Highway (R511)	G2	Traders posted on roadside along northern section.
Hartbeespoort R24 and R560 (Old Rustenburg Road)	C4	Popular weekend market near the Hartbeespoort Dam.
Shades of Ngwenya Glass Factory	E9	View craftspeople making beautiful objects from recycled glass.

Night Activities

CONTACT OR VISIT	TEL NO.	MAP REF	NOTES
Carlton Centre Panorama	(011) 331-1088	H6	Spectacular 360° views of lights of Johannesburg.
Johannesburg Zoological Gardens	(011) 646-2000	H5	Moonlight tours and sleep-overs can be arranged.
Munro Drive Outlook	N/L	H6	Stunning view over the northern suburbs.
Rietvlei Nature Reserve	(012) 345-2274	L7	Night game drives.

Astronomy/Star-Gazing

CONTACT OR VISIT	TEL NO.	MAP REF	NOTES
Aloe Ridge Hotel	(011) 957-2070	D1	Largest telescope in the southern hemisphere; perfect destination for star-gazers.
Old Republic Observatory	(011) 487-1512 telescope.co.za	H6	Monthly lecture and telescopes available.
Planetarium (Wits University)	(011) 717-1390/2	H6	Regular astronomy shows; special weekend programmes for children.
Hartbeeshoek Radio Astronomy Observatory	(012) 326-0742	C3	Monthly public open days; school visits; booking essential.

19th Century San bow and arrow (see page 99)

Natural History Sites

CONTACT OR VISIT	TEL NO.	MAP REF	Authority	Picnic/Braai	Kiosk / Restaurant	Camping	Accommodation	Toilet/Ablution	Wheelchair Access	Children's Recreation	NOTES
Tswaing Crater	(012) 790-2302	J4	Prov	•				•			Meteorite crater 1,4 km i diameter with adjacent eco-museum.
Gladysvale Cave (Contact Dept of Archaeology, Wits University)	(011) 717-1000	B2	Prov								Under excavation; closed public.
Kromdraai Wonder Caves	(011) 957-0106	B2	Pvt	•	•			•			Formed 2 200 million yea guided tours every hour.
Sterkfontein Caves	(011) 956-6342	B2	Prov	•				•			Most famous palaeontolog in South Africa.

The Tswaing meteorite crater (see page 36)

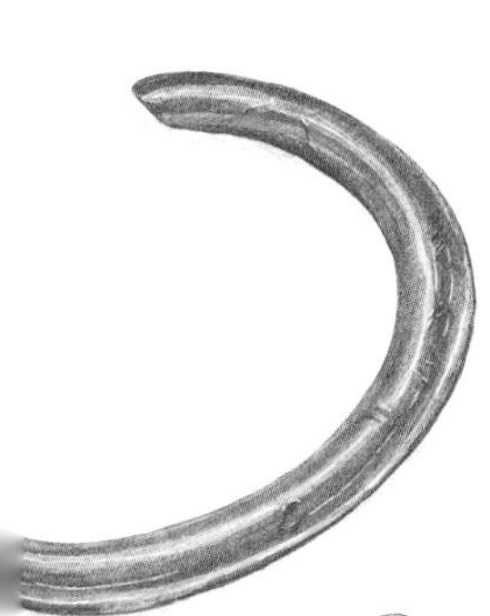

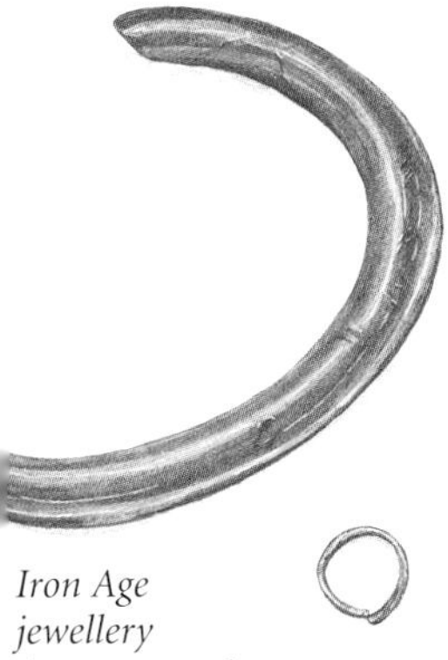

Iron Age jewellery
(see page 101)

Please note that telephone numbers do change. For further information or clarification consult the local telephone directories, or contact 1023 for directory assistance. The publishers welcome feedback from users of these pages. N/L = Not Listed.

The Miriammen Hindu temple in Pretoria

TORICAL SITES MONUMENTS

TACT OR VISIT	TEL NO.	MAP REF	Authority	Picnic/Braai	Kiosk / Restaurant	Camping	Accommodation	Toilet/Ablution	Wheelchair Access	Children's Recreation	NOTES
Reef City	(011) 248-6800	I7	Pvt		•		•	•	•	•	Reproduction of mining town; exhibits; theme park.
or Petersen Square	N/L	F7	Mun						•		Memorial site and photographic exhibits of the Soweto student uprisings of 1976.
dekraal Monument	N/L	C4	Mun					•			Monument to the Voortrekkers; site of annual festivals celebrating trekker history.
rose House	(012) 322-2805	K4	Mun		•			•			Venue for signing of peace treaty ending South African War in 1902.
ammen Temple	N/L	I4	Pvt								Oldest Hindu temple in Pretoria; ornate architecture.
on Buildings	(012) 319-1500	L4	Prov					•	•		Designed by Sir Herbert Baker and built entirely of local sandstone; beautiful grounds.
rtrekker Monument	(012) 326-6770	I5	Mun		•			•			Famous monument celebrating Voortrekker history.

Museums

Morning Glory
(see page 55)

CONTACT OR VISIT	TEL NO.	MAP REF	Authority	Picnic/Braai	Kiosk / Restaurant	Camping	Accommodation	Toilet/Ablution	Wheelchair Access	Children's Recreation	NOTES
Diepkloof Farm Museum	N/L	G4	Mun					•		•	Demonstrations of 19th Century methods.
Vaal Tecnorama Industrial Museum	(016) 450-3136	H7	Mun	•				•	•	•	South Africa's only industrial mus
Kroondal Mill	(014) 536-3614	C6	Pvt		•			•	•		Restored 19th Century flour and mill with restaurant /coffee bar op public.
Lesedi Cultural Village	(012) 205-1394	G6	Pvt		•		•	•	•		Exhibits and live performances de Xhosa, Zulu, Sotho and Pedi cultu meals & accommodation.
Tswaing Crater Museum	(012) 790-2302	J4	Prov					•			Eco-museum at site of vast meteor
Willem Prinsloo Agricultural Museum	(012) 736-2035	L6	Pvt	•	•	•	•	•	•	•	Museum of 19th Century farm life baking and candle-making demon
Adler Museum of the History of Medicine	(011) 489-9432	H6	Pvt					•			Various displays including pharma herbarium & traditional healers' r
Benoni Museum	(011) 741-6231/4	M6	Mun					•			Exhibits of history of gold-mining
Bernberg Museum of Costume	(011) 646-0716	H6	Mun					•			Period costumes (18th – early 20th
Geological Museum	(011) 717-1000	H6	Pvt					•	•		Variety of exhibits; Wits University.
Hechter-Schutze Afro-culture Museum	(011) 894-4535	M7	Pvt	•				•			Cultural life exhibits from Stone A present day; by appointment only.
Museum Africa	(011) 833-5624	H6	Mun		•			•	•		Johannesburg's biggest museum; ex from Stone Age to present day.
Palaeontology Museum (Wits University)	(011) 717-1000	H6	Pvt					•	•		Displays of important prehistoric f dinosaur eggs; open weekdays.
Planetarium	(011) 717-1390/2	H6	Mun					•			Year-round exhibits & educational programmes
Roodepoort City Museum	(011) 472-1400	D5	Mun					•			Photos & objects (pioneer days to
Social Anthropology Museum	(011) 717-1000	H6	Pvt					•			Collections of cultural artefacts (mainly African).
South African Breweries World of Beer	(011) 836-4900	H6	Pvt					•	•		Permanent exhibitions on the histor brewing in South Africa; gift shop & conference centre.
South African National Museum of Military History	(011) 646-5513	H5	Mun		•			•		•	Established 53 years; armoured vehi aeroplanes, Sherman tank; award-w Anglo-Boer War exhibition; official Art Museum; conference facilities
Transport Technology Museum	(011) 435-9718	H7	Mun		•			•			Land transport displays; children's t
Zoology Museum	(011) 717-1000	H6	Pvt					•	•		Wits University; by appointment on
Kruger House Museum	(012) 326-9172	K4	NFI		•			•			Home of Paul Kruger, former SA pr
Museum of Anthropology & Archaeology	(012) 420-2595	K4	Pvt					•	•		At University of Pretoria; variety of of diverse cultures of southern Afric
National Cultural History Museum	(012) 324-6082	K4	Mun					•			Exhibits depicting 2 million years of on the African sub-continent.
Pioneer Open-air Museum	(012) 803-6086	L4	NFI	•	•			•		•	Restored Voortrekker farmhouse; ch educational workshop with booking
Sammy Marks Museum	(012) 803-6158	L4	NFI		•			•			Authentic Victorian mansion set am enormous jacarandas, croquet, guide every hour.
Smuts House Museum	(012) 667-1176	K7	Pvt	•	•	•	•	•	•	•	Preserved home of Jan Smuts, South African statesman; tea garden; beautiful gardens & walks.
South African Museum of Science & Technology	(012) 322-6404	K4	Prov		•			•		•	Fascinating exhibits on everything fr nuclear energy to holograms.
Transvaal Museum	(012) 322-7632	K4	Prov		•		•	•	•		Natural history museum; large perm collection of birds, mammals & fossi

Monkey's Tail (see page 52)

…NICAL GARDENS

…CT OR VISIT	TEL NO.	MAP REF	Authority	Picnic/Braai	Kiosk / Restaurant	Camping	Accommodation	Toilet/Ablution	Wheelchair Access	Children's Recreation	NOTES
…urg Botanical	(011) 888-4928	G5	Mun	•							365 acres; includes roses, herbs & bonsai.
…srand National Gardens	(011) 958-1750	D4	NBI	•	•			•	•		Lovely walks; beautiful waterfall.
…Botanical Gardens	(012) 804-3200	L4	NBI	•	•			•	•		± 1 700 flower species; more than 500 indigenous trees; educational programmes

…OGICAL GARDENS/CAPTIVE ANIMALS

…CT OR VISIT	TEL NO.	MAP REF	AUTH	Picnic/Braai	Kiosk / Restaurant	Camping	Accommodation	Toilet/Ablution	Wheelchair Access	Children's Recreation	NOTES
…burg Zoological	(011) 646-2000	H5	Mun	•	•			•			Wide variety of animals; lovely trees & walkways.
Zoological Pretoria	(012) 328-3265	J4	Pvt	•	•			•	•	•	3 500 species; best zoo in the country.
…Aquarium	(012) 328-3265	J4	Prov		•			•	•	•	Adjoining National Zoo; 300 species of salt- & fresh-water fish.
…rk (Hartbeespoort	(012) 253-1162	B4	Pvt		•			•			Large variety of snakes; also seals & primates; snake-handling performances Sundays & public holidays; seal show; ferry rides.

… AND SMALLER LAKES

…CT OR VISIT	TEL NO.	MAP REF	AUTH	Picnic/Braai	Kiosk / Restaurant	Camping	Accommodation	Toilet/Ablution	Wheelchair Access	Children's Recreation	NOTES
…n	(016) 371-1391	K9	Prov								Popular for fishing & other watersports.
…oort Dam	(014) 572-3174	E7	Prov				•	•			Small dam in central Magaliesberg.
… Dam	N/L	G2	Prov	•			•	•			Part of the Borakololo Nature Reserve.
…Winter Dam	N/L	L2	Mun	•				•		•	Part of Rust de Winter Nature Reserve; watersports.
… Dam	(014) 555-5351	D3	Pvt		•		•		•		Small dam; popular fishing venue.
…g Lake	(011) 899-4499	L7	Mun	•	•			•		•	Watersports; model boats; miniature train.
…ntia Dam	(011) 646-5309	G5	Mun	•				•		•	Includes Johannesburg Botanical Gardens; watersports.
…Lake	N/L	E6	Mun	•	•			•	•	•	Lovely park; small lake; popular weekends.
…on Lake	N/L	J7	Mun	•	•			•		•	65 ha; watersports; minigolf.
…'s Farm	(011) 453-8066	J6	Mun	•	•			•	•	•	44 ha on Jukskei River; short walks.
…Lake (Benoni)	N/L	M6	Mun	•							Popular waterskiing venue.
…e	N/L	H5	Mun	•	•			•	•	•	Paved walkways; rowing boats; tea garden.
…ord Dam	N/L	J2	Prov	•					•		In Onderstepoort Nature Reserve.
…spoort Dam	(012) 253-0266	C4	Prov	•	•	•	•	•		•	Large dam in foothills of Magaliesberg.
… Dam	(012) 345-2274	L7	Mun	•				•	•		Large dam in Rietvlei Nature Reserve with bird hide.

…potted Genet (…ge 91)

Please note that telephone numbers do change. For further information or clarification consult the local telephone directories, or contact 1023 for directory assistance. The publishers welcome feedback from users of these pages. N/L = Not Listed.

Nature Reserves

CONTACT OR VISIT	TEL NO.	MAP REF	Authority	Picnic/Braai	Kiosk / Restaurant	Camping	Accommodation	Toilet/Ablution	Wheelchair Access	Children's Recreation	NOTES
Abe Bailey Nature Reserve	(018) 786-3431	C4	Pvt	•		•	•	•		•	4 200 ha; nature conservatio extensive wetlands; caves.
Boskop Dam Nature Reserve	(018) 298-1330	B6	Prov	•		•		•			2 800 ha; Red Hartebeest; sp zebra.
Smilin Thru	(056) 816-2000	J9	Pvt	•	•	•	•	•	•	•	Resort on banks of Vaal Rive variety of outdoor activities;
Suikerbosrand Nature Reserve	(011) 904-3933	J6	Prov	•				•	•	•	11 583 ha; animals; ideal for
Vaal Dam Nature Reserve	N/L	K9	Prov	•		•		•			350 ha on huge dam; variety recreational activities.
Borakololo Nature Reserve	N/L	M8	Pvt	•			•				Beautiful reserve on Klipvoo less than 2 hrs from Johanne
Bronkhorstspruit Dam Nature Reserve	N/L	G1	Pvt	•		•	•	•		•	1 800 ha; large dam; popular boating and fishing; 6 am-9
Dikhololo Nature Reserve	(012) 277-1200	F3	Pvt	•	•		•	•	•	•	4-wheel-drive game viewing; luxury accommodation.
Jack Scott Nature Reserve	N/L	G8	Mun								2 800 ha; in Magaliesberg.
Mountain Sanctuary Park Nature Reserve	(014) 534-0114	E7	Pvt	•		•	•	•			Day hikes; booking essential.
Rust de Winter Nature Reserve	N/L	L2	Prov	•				•			1 200 ha; on the Elands River
Rustenburg Nature Reserve	(014) 533-2050	B6	NWPB	•		•	•	•			Birdwatching; small game; visi
Vaalkop Dam Nature Reserve	(014) 555-5351	D3	NWPB								Large dam; waterbirds; indiger
Harvey Nature Reserve	N/L	I6	Mun								6 ha on Linksfield Ridge; small
Klipriviersberg Nature Reserve	(011) 680-4153	G8	Mun								600 ha; Voortrekker Boer wa site; guided walks, 2nd & 4th Iron Age ruins.
Kloofendal Nature Reserve	(011) 679-5912	E5	Mun	•							100 ha; walking trails; Septen
Little Falls Nature Reserve	(011) 958-1010	D4	Mun	•				•	•	•	Small reserve; short walking
Melville Koppies Nature Reserve	(011) 888-4831	G6	Mun					•			Iron Age site; many indigeno open 1st & 3rd Sunday 3-6pn Sunday 9am-12pm; Septembe
Norscot Koppies Nature Reserve	(011) 465-2230	G3	Mun	•				•			Short walks.
Pamula Park Nature Reserve	N/L	L5	Mun								Small pan; centrally located.
Rhino & Lion Nature Reserve	(011) 957-0109	C2	Pvt	•	•		•	•		•	1 000 ha; game drives; booking horse trails & mountain biking
Rietfontein Ridge Nature Reserve	N/L	H2	Mun								25 ha; just north of Sandton; walks.
Diepsloot Nature Reserve	(011) 464-1510	F8	Mun								2 600 ha; 40 mins from Johan need permission to enter.
Faerie Glen Nature Reserve	(012) 348-1265	L5	Mun		•			•			100 ha; wide variety of indigen
Groenkloof Nature Reserve	(012) 440-8316	J5	Mun	•			•	•			600 ha; entrance at Fountains camping; mountain biking an trails.
Hartbeespoort Dam Nature Reserve (Oberon)	(012) 244-1353	B4	Prov	•	•	•	•	•		•	Lovely reserve bordering popu
Magaliesberg Protected Natural Environment	N/L	A-K 3-5	Prov	•	•	•	•			•	40 000 ha; stretches from Rust to Pretoria; popular climbing
Onderstepoort Nature Reserve	N/L	I2	Prov	•					•		Large reserve north of Pretori
Rietvlei Nature Reserve	(012) 345-2274	L7	Mun	•				•	•		Many activities; night game dr tours & horse trails.
Roodeplaat Dam Reserve	N/L	M2	Prov	•				•		•	1 695 ha; bird sanctuary; recre activities.
Vergenoeg Nature Reserve	(012) 671-7672	B4	Pvt				•				53 ha; southern slopes of Mag
Wonderboom Nature Reserve	(012) 543-0918	J3	Mun	•				•		•	1 000-year-old fig tree; caves a
Zwartkop Nature Reserve	N/L	I6	Mun	•				•		•	80 ha; bordering Hennops Riv

Elephants
(see page 87)

PARKS/RESERVES

CT OR VISIT	TEL NO.	MAP REF	Authority	Picnic/Braai	Kiosk / Restaurant	Camping	Accommodation	Toilet/Ablution	Wheelchair Access	Children's Recreation	NOTES
Cheetah Centre	(012) 504-1921	H6	Pvt		•			•			Guided tours; breeding programmes.
erg National Park	(014) 555-5351	A2	Prov	•	•	•	•	•	•	•	5 500 ha; adjacent to Sun City; Big 5; Wild Dog; ancient volcanic rock formations.
ge Nature/Game Reserve	(011) 957-2070	D1	Pvt		•		•	•	•		In Swartkop Hills; open landrover viewing.
orp Game Reserve	(011) 665-4342	A4	Pvt	•	•	•	•	•		•	Large selection of game; 4 of the big 5; bird aviary.
ari Park	(011) 460-1814	F2	Pvt	•	•			•		•	± 50 lion; other small game.

S

CT OR VISIT	TEL NO.	MAP REF	Authority	Picnic/Braai	Kiosk / Restaurant	Camping	Accommodation	Toilet/Ablution	Wheelchair Access	Children's Recreation	NOTES
Park	(011) 816-1104	L4	Mun	•	•			•		•	Weekend recreation park; dam; yacht club.
Pioneer Park	N/L	L4	Mun	•							Authentic Dutch windmill; beautiful gardens with fountains.
Park	(011) 899-4157	M7	Mun	•				•		•	Educational park; farm animals.
ark	N/L	M6	Mun	•				•		•	Rabbits & small animals; ideal for children.
rk	(011) 888-4831	G5	Mun	•				•		•	On Braamfontein spruit; houses the Delta Environmental Centre for school groups; parties; adult groups by prior arrangement.
llman Park	(011) 802-3309	H4	Mun	•				•	•	•	Recreational centre; beautiful gardens; sculptures.
ey Pleasure Park	N/L	H8	Mun	•				•		•	Outdoor concert venue; children's play area.
d's Farm	N/L	J5	Mun	•	•			•		•	Lovely park for children.
Park	N/L	H6	Mun		•				•		Johannesburg's oldest park, and home to Johannesburg Art Gallery.
fontein Conservation Conference Centre	(011) 606-2846	J4	Pvt	•				•	•		All activities by appointment only; walks 1 Sat. & 1 Sun. a month and Tuesday. mornings; Environmental interpretation centre; birdwatching.
ark	(011) 463-5773	G3	Pvt		•			•	•	•	Landscaped garden centre; secure varied children's paradise.
Park	N/L	I6	Mun	•	•			•		•	Small dam; facilities for children.
n Field and Study Centre	(011) 783-7407	H4	Mun	•				•		•	Park on Braamfontein Spruit; large trees.
y Lane Animal Farm	(012) 345-2010	K5	Pvt	•	•			•		•	Animal feeding; tractor rides; ideal for children and party venue.
ins Park	N/L	L5	Mun	•		•		•	•	•	Near Pretoria city centre; on Apies River.
ta Park	N/L	L6	Mun	•				•			Popular outdoor music venue.

Ladybird
(see page 56)

Please note that telephone numbers do change. For further information or clarification consult the local telephone directories, or contact 1023 for directory assistance. The publishers welcome feedback from users of these pages. N/L = Not Listed.

Land and Climate

The land represented by the maps in this book is very, very old. Somewhere around 4 thousand million to 3 thousand million years ago the surface of our molten Earth cooled and formed a thin crust of rock. This ancient rock, the Basement Granite, has largely been eroded, but small portions remain at a few sites around the world, including some in Gauteng.

This area was a central portion of an original super-continent that we call Pangea. Pangea divided into the northern Laurasia and the southern Gondwana, with Africa at the centre of the southern landmass. At different times this area was covered by ice, water, sand and vegetation, but bits of its original rock can still be seen today (see page 32).

Further cooling allowed water to condense, creating mineral-rich seas. Then, somewhere in the sun-bathed shallows of the world, the sun's energy was harnessed by the first plant-like organisms. In the process they added oxygen to the existing primitive atmosphere. This laid the foundation for the evolution of other, later forms of Life and of our present climates.

View over Mankwe Dam in the Pilanesberg

Ground Aga
(see page

The Ground Below

The Gauteng we see today is the result of many processes taking place over many thousands of years. The area has been bent and buckled; it has been heated and cooled, bombarded, dried and flooded. How these various happenings affected the land is explained on the following pages.

Volcanic Action

Volcanoes dramatically altered eastern South and this area became part of a huge basin. Water dı into this depression formed a large, shallow inland Between 3 and 2 thousand million years ago materi the surrounding highlands was deposited in the sea, in a layer we call the Black Reef. The rock that was later made of these deposits contains a fine, soft, yellow metal – gold (see box for a more detailed discussion).

Polished segment of Black Reef

Underground mining in Gauteng

ed,
hick layer of
ch dolomite
l the Black Reef.
the dolomite lies in a
east-west band between
esburg and Pretoria.

efore the gold of the Black
as to become important to
kind, water-formed caves in
lomite would provide shelter
earliest ancestors.

he inland sea shallowed.
zite gravels and fine silts
over the dolomite. The sea
ally dried, revealing a flat,
featureless plain. Fossilised
, formed in the sands of the
v sea, can still be seen today
mber of places.

Lime-rich dolomite

Quartz pebbles

Quartzite rock with fossilised ripples

Early miner

The Origin of Gold

One theory is that gold was present in the original rock, the Basement Granite, that lies below the Black Reef. Superheated water percolated from the Basement Granite, up through the Black Reef layers. The extremely hot water lifted the gold out of the lower rock and deposited it in the Black Reef (the Hydrothermal Theory).

Another explanation states that gold was carried into the earliest sea (see opposite) by the streams and rivers eroding the surrounding highlands. The original gold source lay, or may yet lie, elsewhere. The gold we mine today was simply deposited, along with eroded rocks, pebbles and silt, on the bottom of the inland sea (the Placer Theory).

Mountain Building

Two thousand million years ago, to the north of Gauteng, just beneath the surface of the Earth a huge well of lava formed. The rock layers that had been laid down in the inland sea tilted into this lava well. The layers eventually broke under the strain and, after the rubble had been eroded, their edges jutted through the surface as long, parallel, east-west ridges of broken rock. Over time the area was again weathered and eroded by glaciers, droughts and tropical storms.

The Witwatersrand The gold-bearing Black Reef surfaced as the ridge we call the Witwatersrand. Johannesburg lies approximately at the centre of this ridge today. The limestone-based dolomite layer contains no hard, erosion-resistant material, and simply weathered away to form an undulating, flat surface to the north of Johannesburg. The heat of the lava changed some of the rock of the Magaliesberg into the hard, resistant quartzite that forms the mountains today.

Quartz pebbles

Natal Red Top grass (see page 63) plays an important in stabilising soil.

Undulating, flat grasslands in Gaut

Plains Zebra (see page 89)

Hard, resistant quartzite in the Magaliesberg

The Magaliesberg's north slope is more gradual than that on the southern side, and it has fine examples of deep, protected kloofs. Fortunately, their owners strictly control access and use, and have helped to preserve these popular, delicate environments. The entire range has been declared a protected area, in an attempt to curb excessive, disorganised and destructive use.

The Wild Foxglove (see page 55) grows on the slopes of the Magaliesberg.

African White-
kwood, predominant
e kloofs (see page 68)

Gauteng mountains offer a variety of wonderful opportunities for outdoor adventures

Rivers, Craters and Caves

Certain natural features in this area, like the caves and the river drainage pattern, formed gradually over many millions of years. They are the work of the unimagineably slow process of removing material, one microscopic piece at a time. Picnics and hikes in the Gauteng area become more exciting once you understand how the rivers, craters and caves have been formed.

Dolomite Caves

The tilting of the rock layers (see page 32) brought the deep-lying gold to the surface. As important, however, was the surfacing of the dolomite, because this water-soluble rock formed caves, that provided early near-humans with both shelter and refuge. In fact, were it not for these caves, we would probably not know as much as we do about our early ancestors (see grids page 22).

Evidence of early cave dwellers: tortoise shell container and necklace of egg shell beads

Dolomite caves at Sterkfontein, west of Johannesburg

Aerial view of Hartbeespoort Dam

triguing River Drainage Pattern

mous gold-producing Ridge of White Waters (Witwatersrand) ;es the Province of Gauteng roughly from east to west. Part of this orms the Continental Divide watershed for rivers which flow either vards via the Crocodile and Limpopo Rivers to the Indian Ocean, or vards via the Vaal and Orange Rivers to the Atlantic Ocean. Two rain falling side-by-side onto opposite sides of the crest of the main ng block at the Witwatersrand University, may end up in opposite ;! The same happens at nesburg International Airport.

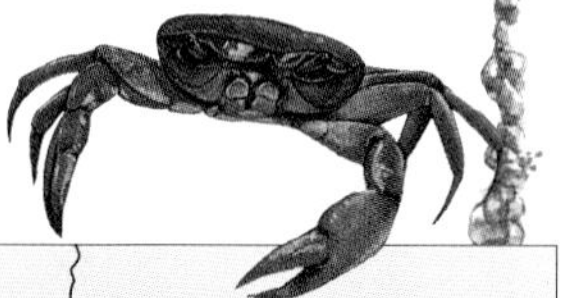

River Crab
(see page 49)

1 50 km of central Johannesburg, -flowing rivers have dropped over etres to Hartebeespoort Dam. owing streams, relatively clean rapids and some waterfalls cterise these rivers. Many mountain , like the Magaliesberg to the north, rovide suitable sites for numerous ssive dams of which the beespoort Dam is the largest.

ntrast, the south-flowing rivers drop one third of this altitude over the 1 to the Vaal River. They are therefore slower flowing, with greater fine ent loads, making the water look for example the Vaal (grey) The slower flow also allows the opment of numerous reed beds, ew or no rapids, as seen in places ne Marievale Bird Sanctuary and okspruit Environmental Centre age 15).

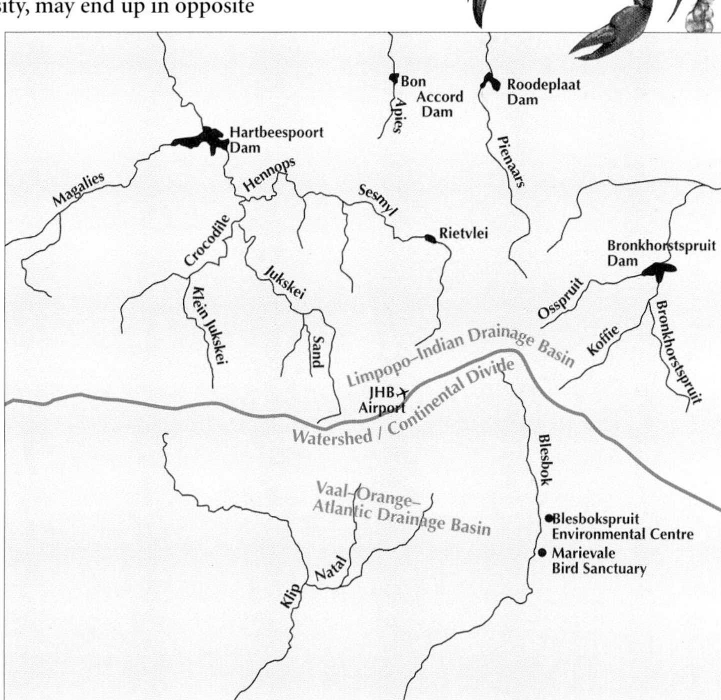

Patterns of river system flowing north and south from the Witwatersrand

iver pebbles

Rivers, Craters and Caves

Other natural features, such as the Tswaing Crater and Pilanesberg, are the result of sudden, cataclysmic events that have left their mark for us to wonder at and ponder over today. Such happenings can change a familiar scene into a foreign landscape in a matter of minutes or days.

Tswaing Crater
Two hundred thousand years ago a meteor crashed to Earth just north of present-day Pretoria. Travelling at around 80 000 km/hr it struck with a force estimated to equal 65 Hiroshima-type atomic bombs. It blasted a crater 120 metres deep, with a 60-metre high surrounding ridge. The 1,2 kilometre-wide crater has a salty lake at its centre, where a salt mine operated earlier this century. However, the many scattered stone tools document a far longer history of human activity. The Tswaing Enviro-museum has been established at the crater, with the help of the Transvaal Museum, Pretoria.

Coarse crys

The massive Tswaing Crater

Stone tools

Circle of mountains surrounding Pilanesberg

Pilanesberg

Between about 1,4 thousand million and 1,2 thousand million years ago, pressure began to build within the Earth, just north of where Rustenburg lies today. Eventually a raised dome of earth and rock exploded, creating a remarkably circular series of cracks, faults and rocky ridges – the Pilanesberg. The feature rises suddenly from a flat surrounding plain, and covers an area of 500 km². This volcano is the second-largest of the very rare alkaline volcanoes in the world. Today these circles of mountains naturally protect the Pilanesberg National Park and its several leisure resorts (see page 27).

-ella Acacia
-age 61)

Pilanesberg National Park

Giraffe (see page 87)

The Air Above

Gauteng is predominantly flat, and the land surface is very strongly heated by the summer sun. Air above the ground is also heated, and begins to rise. The more strongly it is heated, the more quickly it will rise. Although most cloud types form in horizontal layers, 90% of the clouds in this area form vertically, on top of these rising columns of air. Air will continue to rise while it is sufficiently warm, and may reach speeds of 30m/sec (110 km/hr). Over Gauteng the clouds formed in this way may reach a height of 13 kilometres (40 000 feet). The temperatures of the vertical cloud are usually about 10°C at the base, and -50°C at the top. Within these huge, towering piles of beautiful cloud, several interesting processes are taking place.

Storm

Bullfrog (see page 45), found in recently flooded grasslands

Rain

All air contains invisible water vapour. When warm air cools sufficiently, some of this gaseous vapour changes into liquid, and becomes visible as cloud or dew. Warm, rising air changes to cloud at a height called the Condensation Level. This height varies from 0 metres (dew) to many thousands of metres, according to the amount of vapour and the general temperature. As more vapour reaches this level, more and more liquid accumulates. The droplets of water begin to join, getting bigger and bigger. When they become too big for the rising air to support them, they fall back to Earth as rain.

Common Caco (see page 45), frequently seen after rain

Hail

Above the Condensation Level (see Rain), there is a still colder level, the Freezing Level. If the rising curren are warm enough, and therefore strong enough, they can rise to the Freezing Level. Here, the drops of wate they are carrying freeze, and become hailstones. Additional water from below will freeze onto existing hailstones, making them bigger and heavier. When the rising air can no longer support them, they fall to Ea causing hail damage according to their size.

ıtic lightning over Johannesburg

ghtning and Thunder

e movement of the various particles within a cloud, such as dust and hailstones, oduces static electricity. When the cloud is big enough, the electrical charges oduce lightning. The top of a storm cloud can become either positively or negatively arged. The base then takes on the opposite charge. This charge at the cloud base luces its opposite charge on the ground below the cloud. Eventually the fireworks ırt. Huge lightning bolts jump between the differently charged areas, at speeds ound 90 000 km/hr. If they remain within the cloud, we see sheet lightning. scharges to and from the ground are called forked lightning, while streak lightning shes from cloud to cloud. Gauteng receives 7,5 strikes per km^2 per year – one of the ghest lightning strike-rates in the world.

The Hamerkop, Scopus umbretta (56 cm), also known as the Lightning Bird, whose presence is believed by some tribes to precede lightning storms

ıunder is the sound of super-heated air panding as the lightning bolt passes through while, if you are close enough to hear it, the ack' is the sound of the bolt itself. The ımber of seconds between seeing the flash and aring the thunder tells how far away the htning is: about 350 metres for each second.

ew and Frost

n still, quiet, clear nights the Earth's surface ols quickly as it gets rid of its daytime heat to space. Water vapour in the air next to the ound, around plants, and against metal jects, condenses, and collects as dew. This ocess can occur in both summer and winter, though in winter, with the lower temperatures, e dew may freeze into frost.

Early morning dew

THE PLANT COVERING

Plants were the first life forms on the surface of the planet. Able to store energy in the form of light, they flourish wherever temperature and sunlight make it possible. Local conditions of moisture, light and temperature determine which plants will grow where. Temporary and sudden phenomena such as fire and drought, as well as animal browsing and grazing patterns, and humans, also have an important effect on how plants adapt and grow.

Vegetation Zones

Seasonal temperatures and fire greatly affect the form, characteristics and distribution of indigenous grasses, plants, shrubs and trees. Natural fires result from lightning and from spontaneous combustion, but humans are sometimes also responsible.

Different means by which plants disperse their seeds:

Kiaat Bloodwood pods (left) and Large-fruited Bushwillow pods (right) are shaped for wind dispersal.

Typical Highveld landscape – rocky outcrops and open, exposed grassland

e open plains trees that grow are fire-hardy with thick, corky or fire protection. More tender s grow in groups, or among or against the sides of ridges to emselves protection. Trees have volved ingenious ways of ing that their seeds reach, and nate in, the most suitable ts. Seeds are designed to be tributed by wind or water, in irds and animals, or by hooking onto fur or cloth. Their objective is to arrive where temperature, shelter, moisture and nutriments are present in the best combination.

Seeds of Umbrella Acacia (see page 61) are dispersed after animals feed on the pods.

Highveld Protea (see page 62) rely on fire for seed dispersal. The cones are e-resistant, but are ctivated to open after ire when there is little ompetition for the seeds.

The Highveld Cabbage-tree is ideally suited to surviving grass fires (see page 59).

uteng is a summer rainfall area. Johannesburg is about 1 700 metres above sea level, and toria lies at about 1 250 metres. The difference in altitude accounts for Pretoria usually ng about 3°C warmer than Johannesburg. Average rainfall is higher in Johannesburg, ause it is closer to the condensation level, so that condensation occurs more readily.

erage Rain (measured in millimetres)

	J	F	M	A	M	J	J	A	S	O	N	D
)	125	90	91	54	13	9	4	6	27	72	117	105
ı	136	75	82	51	13	7	3	6	22	71	98	110

erage Minimum and Maximum Temperatures (measured in degrees centigrade)

	J	F	M	A	M	J	J	A	S	O	N	D
)	14.7	14.1	13.1	10.3	7.2	4.1	4.1	6.2	9.3	11.2	12.7	13.9
	25.6	25.1	24	21.1	18.9	16	16.7	19.4	22.8	23.8	24.2	25.2
a	17.5	17.2	16	12.2	7.8	4.5	4.5	7.6	11.7	14.2	15.7	16.8
	28.6	28	27	24.1	21.9	19.1	19.6	22.2	25.5	26.6	27.1	28

erage Sunshine (hours per day without cloud)

	J	F	M	A	M	J	J	A	S	O	N	D
b / Pta	8.1	8.0	7.7	7.9	8.9	8.9	9.2	9.2	9.4	8.7	8.3	8.5

erage Daylight (hours per day)

	J	F	M	A	M	J	J	A	S	O	N	D
b / Pta	13.5	13	12.25	11.5	11	10.75	11	11.25	12	12.75	13	13.5

The sound of cicadas (see page 69) is evocative of hot African summer days.

Fish, Amphibians and Reptiles

Plants draw energy directly from the Sun. As the first form of life, they started growing in the planet's early seas. It was then only a matter of time before tiny plant-eating animals evolved. Animal-eating animals were next to make their appearance, and, in water, the stage was set for the whole multitude of life forms that exists on Earth today.

Fish probably evolved first in the sea, then later colonised the freshwater streams, rivers and lakes. As competition for food and living space increased, they explored adjoining land, and developed the characteristics of amphibians.

Only when the amphibians had solved the environmental problems associated with land life did they slowly change into reptiles. First as lizards, then as snakes, they preserved many of the survival techniques developed by their amphibian ancestors.

Fish, amphibians and reptiles are measured in length (L) from tip of nose to tip of tail.

Crocodile River bend, the home for many fish, amphibians and reptiles.

Fish and Amphibians

Fish function underwater just as the animals do on land. There are grazers and browsers of plants, as well as carnivorous hunters, stalking and catching the plant-eating herbivores. Fish eat, breathe and reproduce in water. They are totally dependent on it.

Amphibians show the characteristics needed for both water and land life. The more water-dependent types are covered in a slime, used to keep their skin moist and supple. Toads can survive for long periods without water, but they are not independent of it. Frogs must return to water to lay their soft-shelled, transparent eggs, and water also provides shelter and sustenance for tadpoles.

Water is to fish what air is to animals. Keep it free of harmful chemicals and garbage.

▲ Sharp-toothed Catfish (Barbel) ▼
Clarias gariepinus
(1,4 m; 60 kg)
This remarkable fish prefers flooded areas, and st or slow-moving water. It can breathe air, and ther can move from one body of water to another by w on its front fins. Its diet is truly omnivorous, rang from plants and micro-organisms, through fish, i and larvae, to birds, rodents and carrion. In turn, eaten by many animals, among them Fish Eagles (see page 83), leopards (see page 90), crocodiles and humans.

◄ Banded Tilapia
Tilapia sparrmanii
(23 cm; 0,6 kg)

Red-nosed Mudfish ▼
Labeo rosae (41 cm; 3 kg)
Whether in a dam or a river, this fish will be found only where the bottom is sandy. It eats small organisms, algae, and organic matter it finds along the bottom. At breeding time it migrates up flooding rivers, even over weirs, waterfalls and rapids.

Tilapia live in a variety of habitats, although all prefer more stagnant water. **Banded Tilapia** live under surface plants, and feed on small fish, insects and plants. The **Mozambique Tilapia**, although not indigenous to Gauteng, is now one of the most widespread freshwater fishes in the province. Both construct saucer-shaped nests in the sand, which are often visible from the surface, or if the pool dries up.

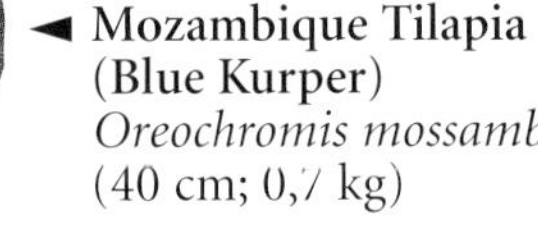

◄ Mozambique Tilapia (Blue Kurper)
Oreochromis mossambi
(40 cm; 0,7 kg)

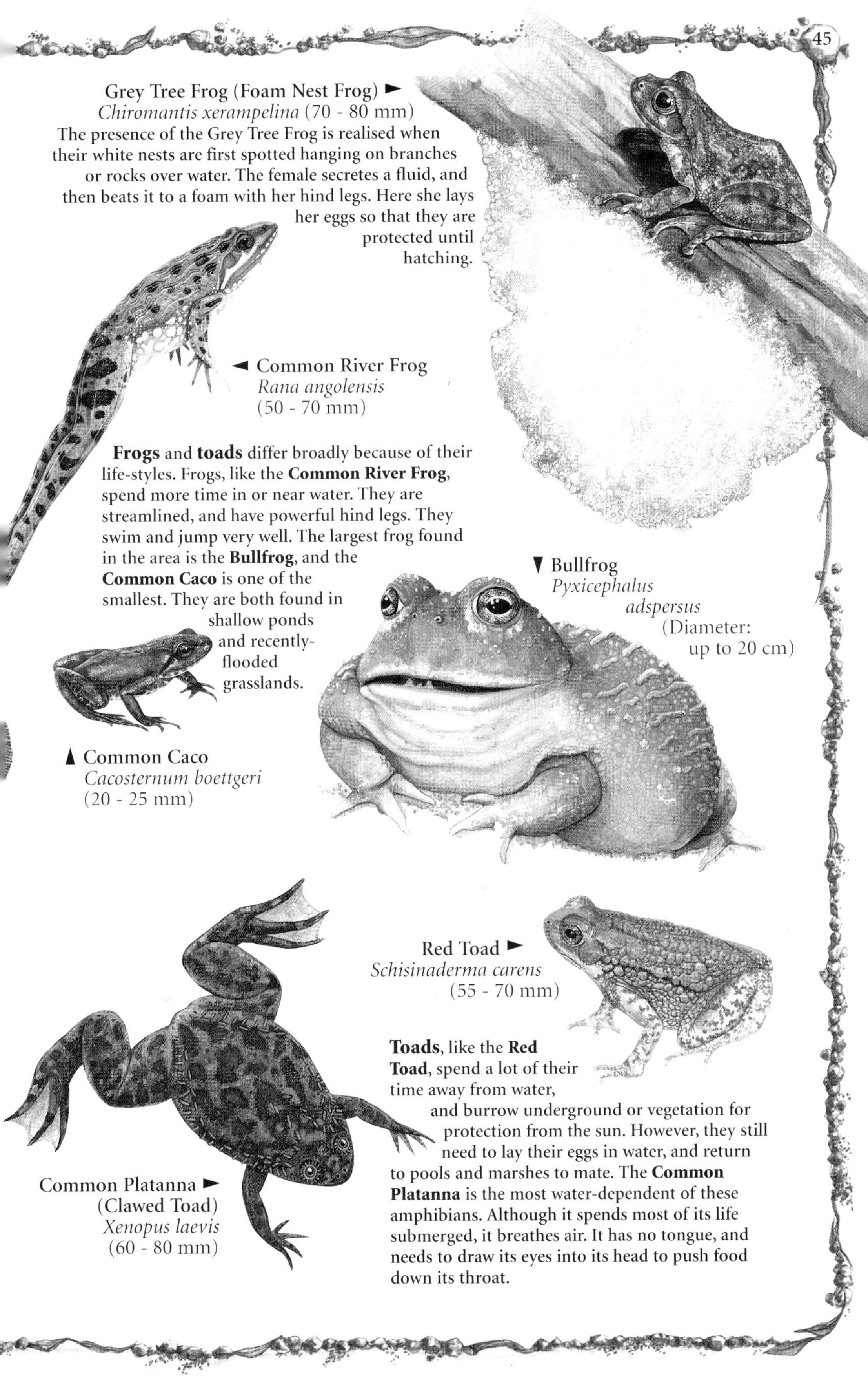

Grey Tree Frog (Foam Nest Frog) ►
Chiromantis xerampelina (70 - 80 mm)
The presence of the Grey Tree Frog is realised when their white nests are first spotted hanging on branches or rocks over water. The female secretes a fluid, and then beats it to a foam with her hind legs. Here she lays her eggs so that they are protected until hatching.

◄ Common River Frog
Rana angolensis
(50 - 70 mm)

Frogs and **toads** differ broadly because of their life-styles. Frogs, like the **Common River Frog**, spend more time in or near water. They are streamlined, and have powerful hind legs. They swim and jump very well. The largest frog found in the area is the **Bullfrog**, and the **Common Caco** is one of the smallest. They are both found in shallow ponds and recently-flooded grasslands.

▼ Bullfrog
Pyxicephalus adspersus
(Diameter: up to 20 cm)

▲ Common Caco
Cacosternum boettgeri
(20 - 25 mm)

Red Toad ►
Schisinaderma carens
(55 - 70 mm)

Toads, like the **Red Toad**, spend a lot of their time away from water, and burrow underground or vegetation for protection from the sun. However, they still need to lay their eggs in water, and return to pools and marshes to mate. The **Common Platanna** is the most water-dependent of these amphibians. Although it spends most of its life submerged, it breathes air. It has no tongue, and needs to draw its eyes into its head to push food down its throat.

Common Platanna ►
(Clawed Toad)
Xenopus laevis
(60 - 80 mm)

Snakes

Snakes are often not the most popular creatures because of their appearance and behaviour, but their diversity exceeds that of mammals in southern Africa. They are highly efficient predators and have evolved amazing adaptations. Some have striking colouration for camouflage; some secrete venom to poison their prey; and others can dislocate their lower jaws in order to swallow large prey whole.

Snakes, like all reptiles, are ectotherms, meaning they control their body temperatures by external means, that is from the sun. The advantage is that reptiles do not have to eat as much food as warm-blooded animals. Many snakes can survive and grow on very little sustenance.

The vast majority of our snakes, and all our lizards, are not poisonous and are therefore totally harmless. In fact they do a great deal of good in controlling rodents. Snakes, like most animals, are only dangerous when you threaten them.

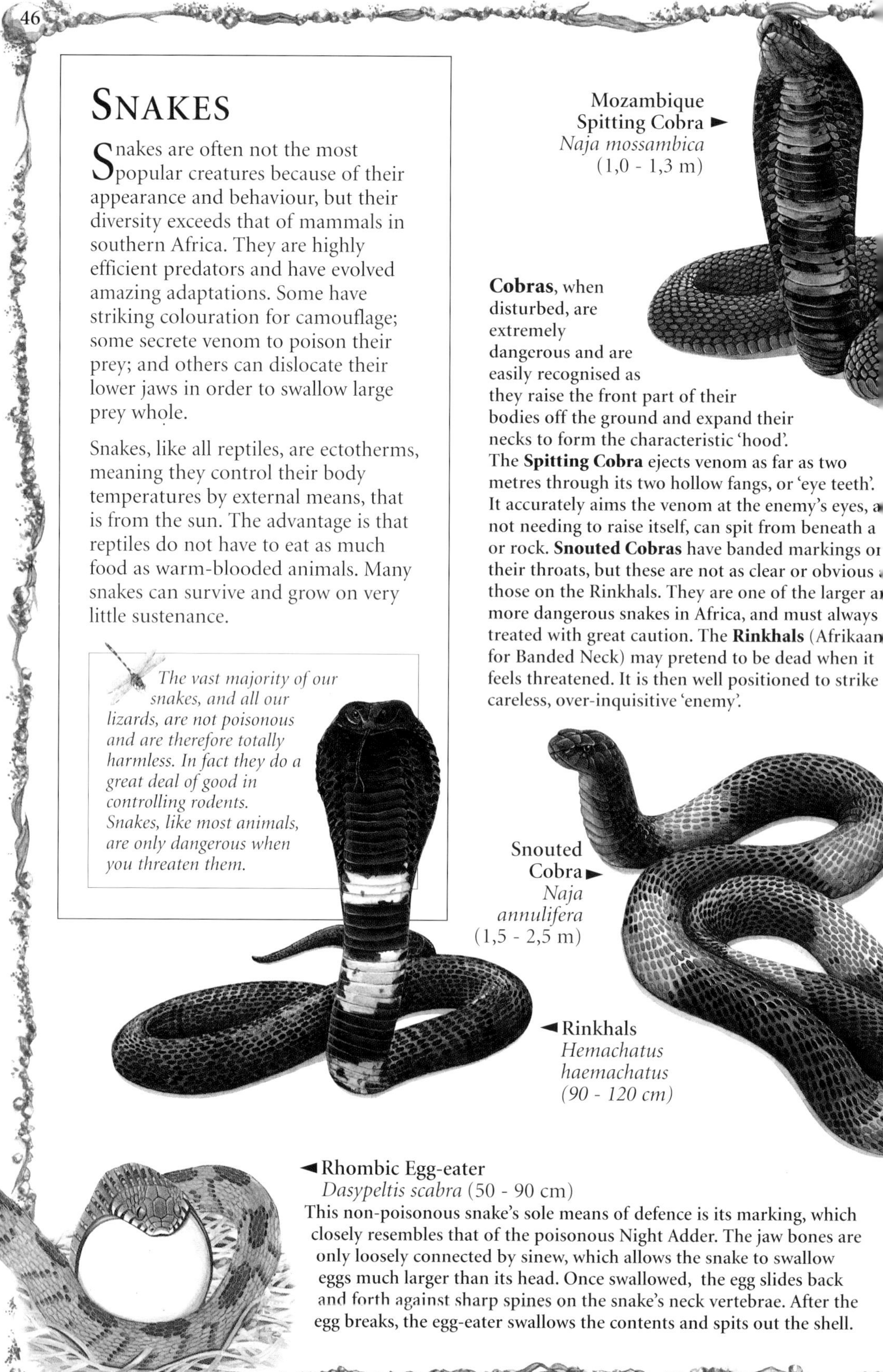

Mozambique Spitting Cobra ►
Naja mossambica
(1,0 - 1,3 m)

Cobras, when disturbed, are extremely dangerous and are easily recognised as they raise the front part of their bodies off the ground and expand their necks to form the characteristic 'hood'. The **Spitting Cobra** ejects venom as far as two metres through its two hollow fangs, or 'eye teeth'. It accurately aims the venom at the enemy's eyes, a not needing to raise itself, can spit from beneath a or rock. **Snouted Cobras** have banded markings o their throats, but these are not as clear or obvious those on the Rinkhals. They are one of the larger a more dangerous snakes in Africa, and must always treated with great caution. The **Rinkhals** (Afrikaan for Banded Neck) may pretend to be dead when it feels threatened. It is then well positioned to strike careless, over-inquisitive 'enemy'.

Snouted Cobra ►
Naja annulifera
(1,5 - 2,5 m)

◄ Rinkhals
Hemachatus haemachatus
(90 - 120 cm)

◄ Rhombic Egg-eater
Dasypeltis scabra (50 - 90 cm)

This non-poisonous snake's sole means of defence is its marking, which closely resembles that of the poisonous Night Adder. The jaw bones are only loosely connected by sinew, which allows the snake to swallow eggs much larger than its head. Once swallowed, the egg slides back and forth against sharp spines on the snake's neck vertebrae. After the egg breaks, the egg-eater swallows the contents and spits out the shell.

Mole Snake ►
Pseudaspis cana (1 - 2 m)
The Mole Snake is not poisonous but will readily strike and bite when cornered. It is one of the few snake species in the world whose males fight seriously at mating time. The adult's diet consists of rats, mice and moles, and it was therefore one of the first snakes to be protected by law in South Africa.

Feeding on a mole rat

▼ Puffadder
Bitis arietans (60 - 100 cm)
This common snake with its characteristic flattened, triangular head is difficult to see. It hunts by ambush, and is responsible for many bites which can be fatal to humans. When people unknowingly step too close to it, it strikes in self-defence. It eats rodents like the Striped Mouse (see page 75), which it bites and immediately releases. It then sluggishly follows the scent to where the animal has died, and swallows it.

mmon Brown Water Snake ►
Lycodonomorphus rufulus
(60 - 80 cm)
The Brown Water Snake is nocturnal, inhabiting moist areas like pans and wetlands. It hunts for frogs and tadpoles, killing them by nstriction. It is harmless to humans and can become very tame.

Catching a frog

◄ Rhombic Skaapsteker (Spotted Skaapsteker)
Psammophylax rhombeatus
(80 - 120 cm)
The Rhombic Skaapsteker is not a dangerous snake but it may bite. It prefers moist grasslands where it hunts for small vertebrates by day. It looks after it eggs by coiling around them until the young have hatched.

Other Reptiles

Unlike amphibians (see page 45), reptiles have dry, horny skin and can be independent of water. They occupy habitats from lush rainforests to the driest deserts. They lay eggs with hard, waterproof shells that keep the developing embryos in a watery environment until they hatch. The more aquatic reptiles, like the Helmeted Terrapin, have soft-shelled eggs and lay them in moist soil.

Although some lizards are legless and may be mistaken for snakes, they differ from snakes in many ways. Lizards usually have movable eyelids and external ear openings on the sides of their heads. However, just to be confusing, geckos are lizards despite not having eyelids, and they clean their eyes with their tongues! Lizards have tapering tails that tend to be even longer than their bodies.

Snakes can be traced back many millions of years, but lizards are even older. Lizard-like reptiles can be seen in 190-million-year-old fossils, long before we find any records of snakes. Some snakes still have small claws marking the place where they used to have legs.

◄ Praying Mantis
Sphodromantis gastrica
Insect (85 mm)

Catching a Praying Mantis

▲ **Flap-neck Chameleon**
Chamaeleo dilepis (20 - 24

Like all chameleons, the Flap-neck Chameleon cat insects by 'spitting' its long, sticky-tipped tongu them. A special circular tongue-muscle surroun slippery bone attached to the floor of its mo When the muscle contracts the tongue shoots out chameleons have grasping tails and rotating eyes, can change colour to match their surroundi

◄ Ground Aga
Agama acul
(15 - 22 cm

(F)

This rough-sc agama uses camouflage to blend with the low rocks and gravel-covered surfaces where it lives. Breeding males, however, perch obvious vantage points, and threaten each other by bobbing their colourful heads. Their diet consists of insects, ants and termites. None of the South African agamas are poisonous.

(M)

Underside

◄ Cape Dwarf Gecko ▼
Lygodactylus capensis
(60 - 70 mm)

This is one of our smaller lizards and, like the skinks, is capable of shedding and re-growing its tail. The Cape Gecko is one of the 'sticky-fingered' geckoes, and can easily walk up a window pane. Although it is active mainly during the day, it may wait on a wall or ceiling at night for insects to be attracted to a light.

▼ Cape Sk
Mabuya capensis (20 - 25 c

Skinks are able to discard their tails, wh continue to wriggle aroun distract predators. Amazingly, new t complete with scales, colours and ner quickly grow again. The Cape Skink lays a clutc tough, soft-shelled eggs, which protect the embryos if climatic conditions are too harsh.

▲ River Crab
Potomonautes perlatus
Crustacean (12 - 15 cm)

Monitors are the largest of the world's lizards. The larger **Nile Monitor** hunts live fish, crabs and frogs. Both lizards use their long, strong claws to rip open termite mounds, and then lay their eggs in the active nests. After the termites have repaired the hole, the eggs incubate safely within. The **Rock Monitor** feeds on beetles, millipedes (see page 65) and grasshoppers, and will even take carrion when it is available.

▼ Nile Monitor ►
Varanus niloticus
(1,0 - 1,4 m)

▼ Rock Monitor
Varanus exanthematicus albigularis
(0,7 - 1,1 m)

▼ Helmeted (Marsh) Terrapin
Pelomedusa subrufa
(Diam: 25 cm; 2,5 kg)

Tortoises and terrapins **fold their necks to draw their heads into their shells**. Tortoises fold theirs vertically, while terrapins fold them sidewise. The **Helmeted Terrapin** looks like a flattened tortoise, and feeds on anything from water plants to carrion. The **Leopard Tortoise**, the largest and widest-ranging tortoise in southern Africa, is not indigenous to Gauteng – the population probably consists of released and escaped pets. The young hatch from the buried eggs after a ground-softening rain.

▲ Leopard Tortoise
Geochelone pardalis
(30 - 55 cm)

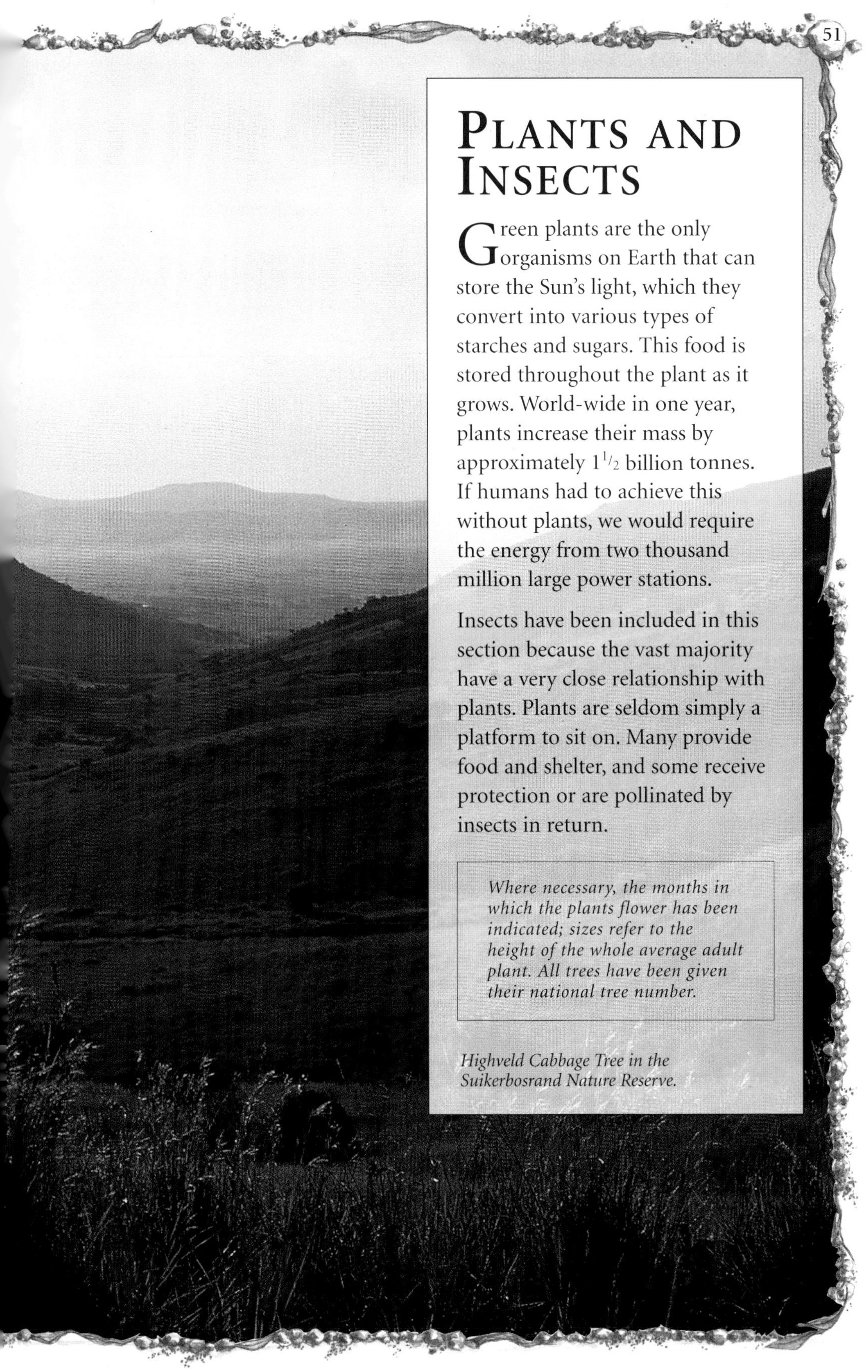

Plants and Insects

Green plants are the only organisms on Earth that can store the Sun's light, which they convert into various types of starches and sugars. This food is stored throughout the plant as it grows. World-wide in one year, plants increase their mass by approximately $1^1/_2$ billion tonnes. If humans had to achieve this without plants, we would require the energy from two thousand million large power stations.

Insects have been included in this section because the vast majority have a very close relationship with plants. Plants are seldom simply a platform to sit on. Many provide food and shelter, and some receive protection or are pollinated by insects in return.

Where necessary, the months in which the plants flower has been indicated; sizes refer to the height of the whole average adult plant. All trees have been given their national tree number.

Highveld Cabbage Tree in the Suikerbosrand Nature Reserve.

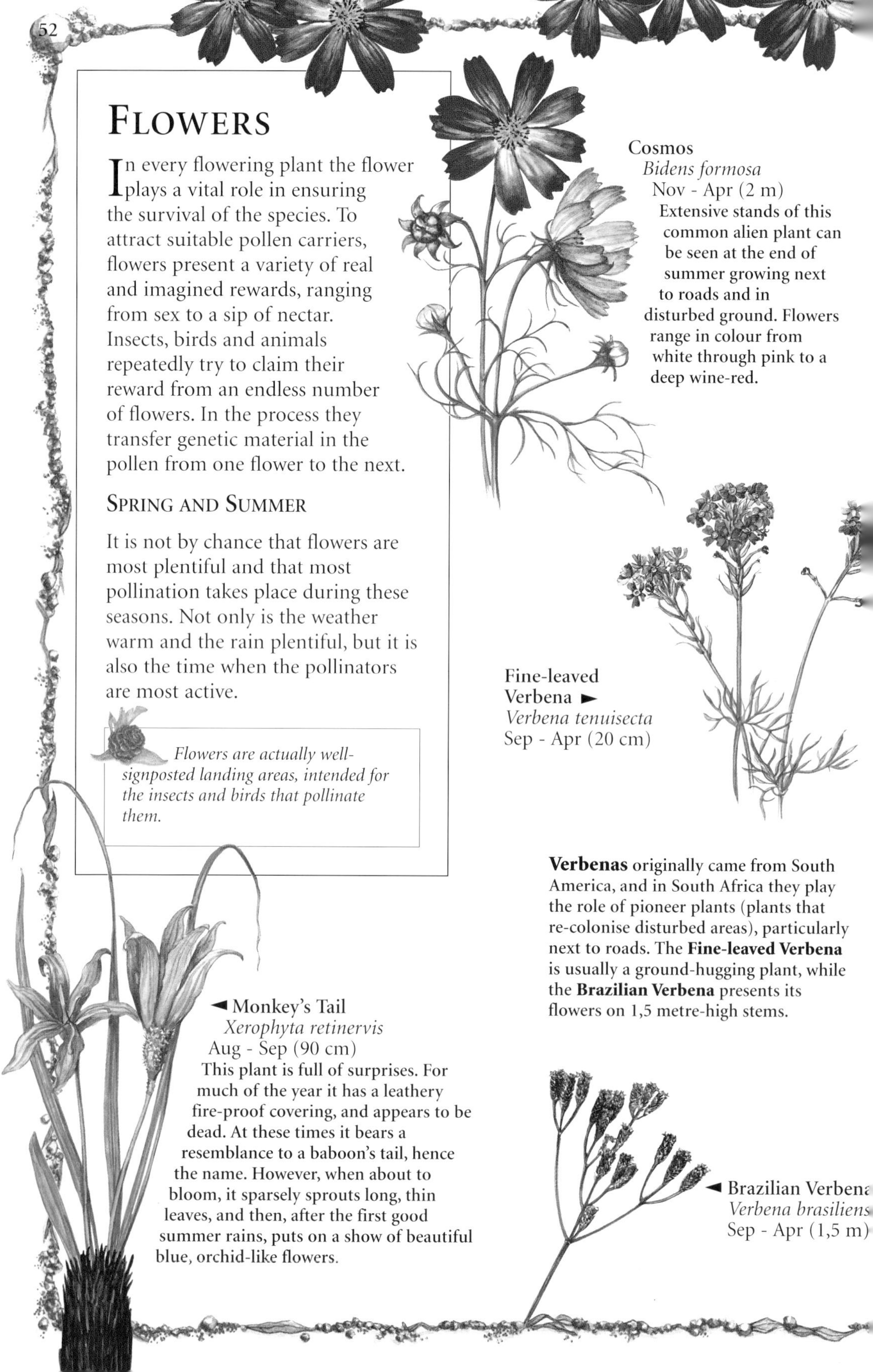

FLOWERS

In every flowering plant the flower plays a vital role in ensuring the survival of the species. To attract suitable pollen carriers, flowers present a variety of real and imagined rewards, ranging from sex to a sip of nectar. Insects, birds and animals repeatedly try to claim their reward from an endless number of flowers. In the process they transfer genetic material in the pollen from one flower to the next.

SPRING AND SUMMER

It is not by chance that flowers are most plentiful and that most pollination takes place during these seasons. Not only is the weather warm and the rain plentiful, but it is also the time when the pollinators are most active.

Flowers are actually well-signposted landing areas, intended for the insects and birds that pollinate them.

Cosmos
Bidens formosa
Nov - Apr (2 m)
Extensive stands of this common alien plant can be seen at the end of summer growing next to roads and in disturbed ground. Flowers range in colour from white through pink to a deep wine-red.

Fine-leaved Verbena ►
Verbena tenuisecta
Sep - Apr (20 cm)

Verbenas originally came from South America, and in South Africa they play the role of pioneer plants (plants that re-colonise disturbed areas), particularly next to roads. The **Fine-leaved Verbena** is usually a ground-hugging plant, while the **Brazilian Verbena** presents its flowers on 1,5 metre-high stems.

◄ Monkey's Tail
Xerophyta retinervis
Aug - Sep (90 cm)
This plant is full of surprises. For much of the year it has a leathery fire-proof covering, and appears to be dead. At these times it bears a resemblance to a baboon's tail, hence the name. However, when about to bloom, it sparsely sprouts long, thin leaves, and then, after the first good summer rains, puts on a show of beautiful blue, orchid-like flowers.

◄ Brazilian Verbena
Verbena brasiliensis
Sep - Apr (1,5 m)

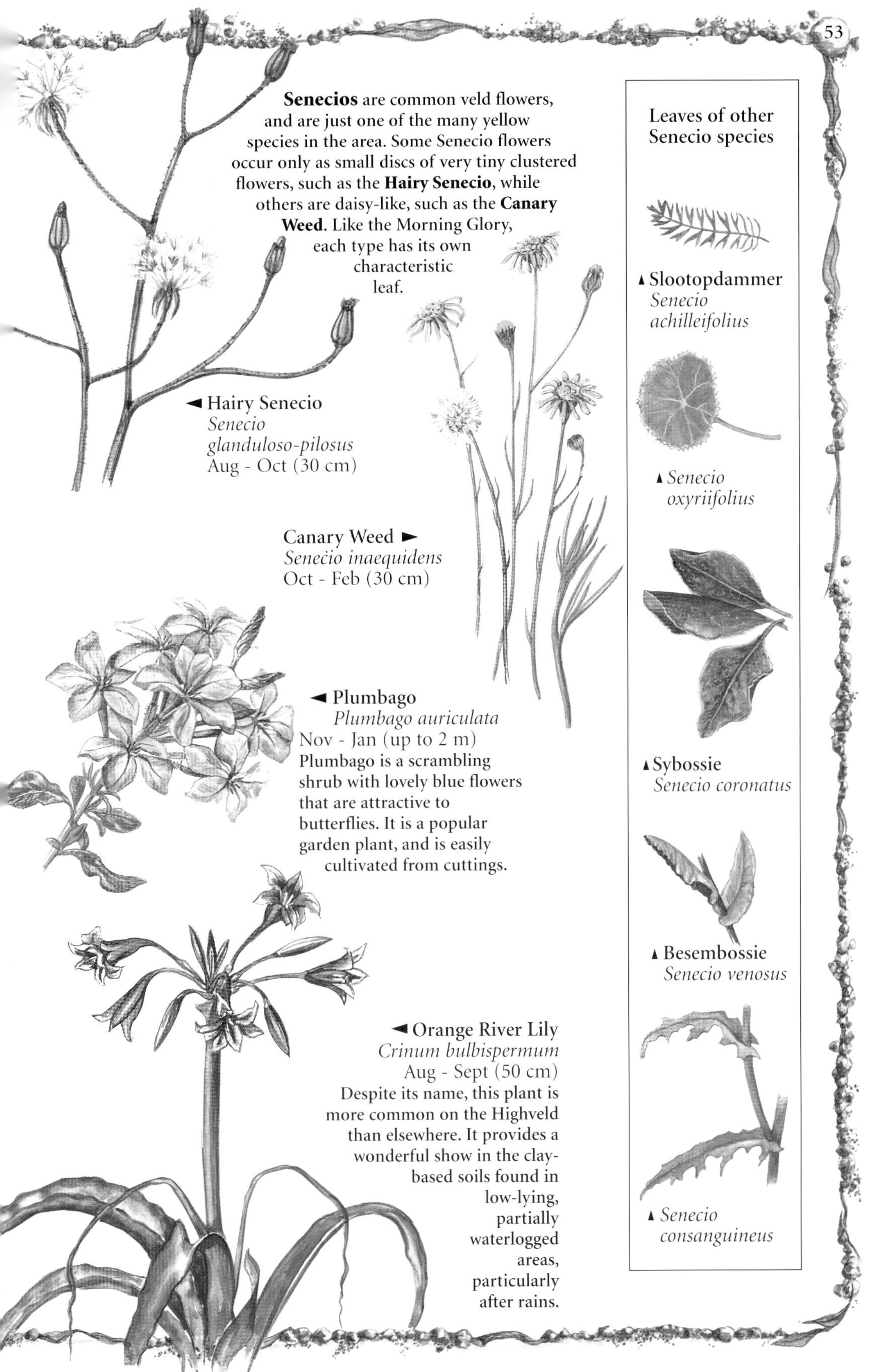

Senecios are common veld flowers, and are just one of the many yellow species in the area. Some Senecio flowers occur only as small discs of very tiny clustered flowers, such as the **Hairy Senecio**, while others are daisy-like, such as the **Canary Weed**. Like the Morning Glory, each type has its own characteristic leaf.

◄ Hairy Senecio
Senecio glanduloso-pilosus
Aug - Oct (30 cm)

Canary Weed ►
Senecio inaequidens
Oct - Feb (30 cm)

◄ **Plumbago**
Plumbago auriculata
Nov - Jan (up to 2 m)
Plumbago is a scrambling shrub with lovely blue flowers that are attractive to butterflies. It is a popular garden plant, and is easily cultivated from cuttings.

◄ **Orange River Lily**
Crinum bulbispermum
Aug - Sept (50 cm)
Despite its name, this plant is more common on the Highveld than elsewhere. It provides a wonderful show in the clay-based soils found in low-lying, partially waterlogged areas, particularly after rains.

Leaves of other Senecio species

▲ **Slootopdammer**
Senecio achilleifolius

▲ *Senecio oxyriifolius*

▲ **Sybossie**
Senecio coronatus

▲ **Besembossie**
Senecio venosus

▲ *Senecio consanguineus*

Flowers

Medicinal and Poisonous Flowers

Defence chemicals produced by a plant may be bad tasting, and in stronger doses may cause discomfort or even death. Brushing some plants that are hairy or covered in tiny thorns may cause itchy rashes or painful stings. Very small quantities of many of these poisons have been found to have powerful medicinal properties. Our human ancestors discovered and verified the medicinal or poisonous properties of plants, very cautiously over very long periods of time.

Do not eat unfamiliar plants, or listen to self-proclaimed 'experts', as some earlier people might have done to their cost!

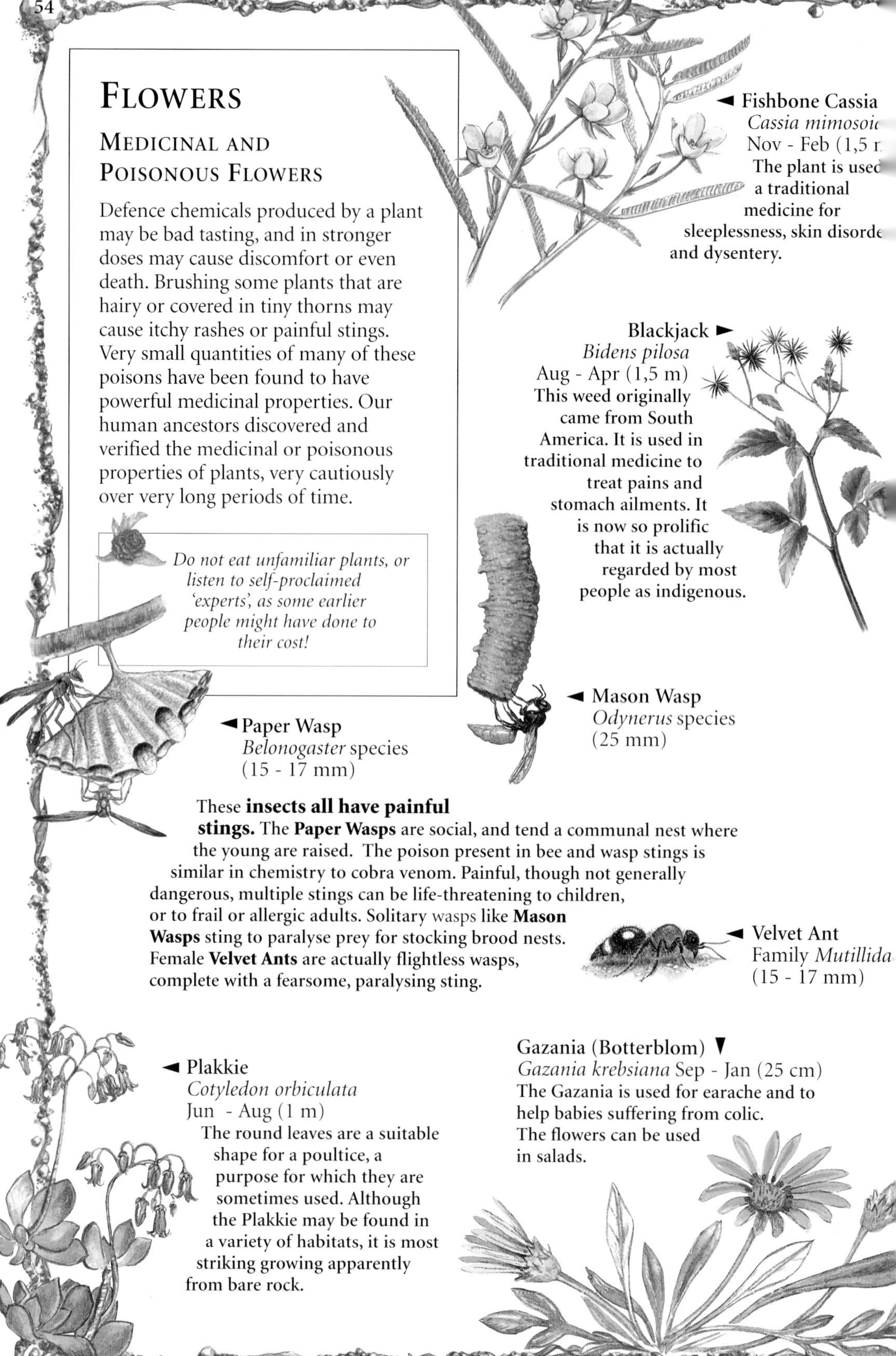

◄ **Fishbone Cassia**
Cassia mimosoi
Nov - Feb (1,5 r
The plant is used a traditional medicine for sleeplessness, skin disord and dysentery.

Blackjack ►
Bidens pilosa
Aug - Apr (1,5 m)
This weed originally came from South America. It is used in traditional medicine to treat pains and stomach ailments. It is now so prolific that it is actually regarded by most people as indigenous.

◄ Mason Wasp
Odynerus species
(25 mm)

◄ Paper Wasp
Belonogaster species
(15 - 17 mm)

These **insects all have painful stings.** The **Paper Wasps** are social, and tend a communal nest where the young are raised. The poison present in bee and wasp stings is similar in chemistry to cobra venom. Painful, though not generally dangerous, multiple stings can be life-threatening to children, or to frail or allergic adults. Solitary wasps like **Mason Wasps** sting to paralyse prey for stocking brood nests. Female **Velvet Ants** are actually flightless wasps, complete with a fearsome, paralysing sting.

◄ Velvet Ant
Family *Mutillida*
(15 - 17 mm)

◄ Plakkie
Cotyledon orbiculata
Jun - Aug (1 m)
The round leaves are a suitable shape for a poultice, a purpose for which they are sometimes used. Although the Plakkie may be found in a variety of habitats, it is most striking growing apparently from bare rock.

Gazania (Botterblom) ▼
Gazania krebsiana Sep - Jan (25 cm)
The Gazania is used for earache and to help babies suffering from colic. The flowers can be used in salads.

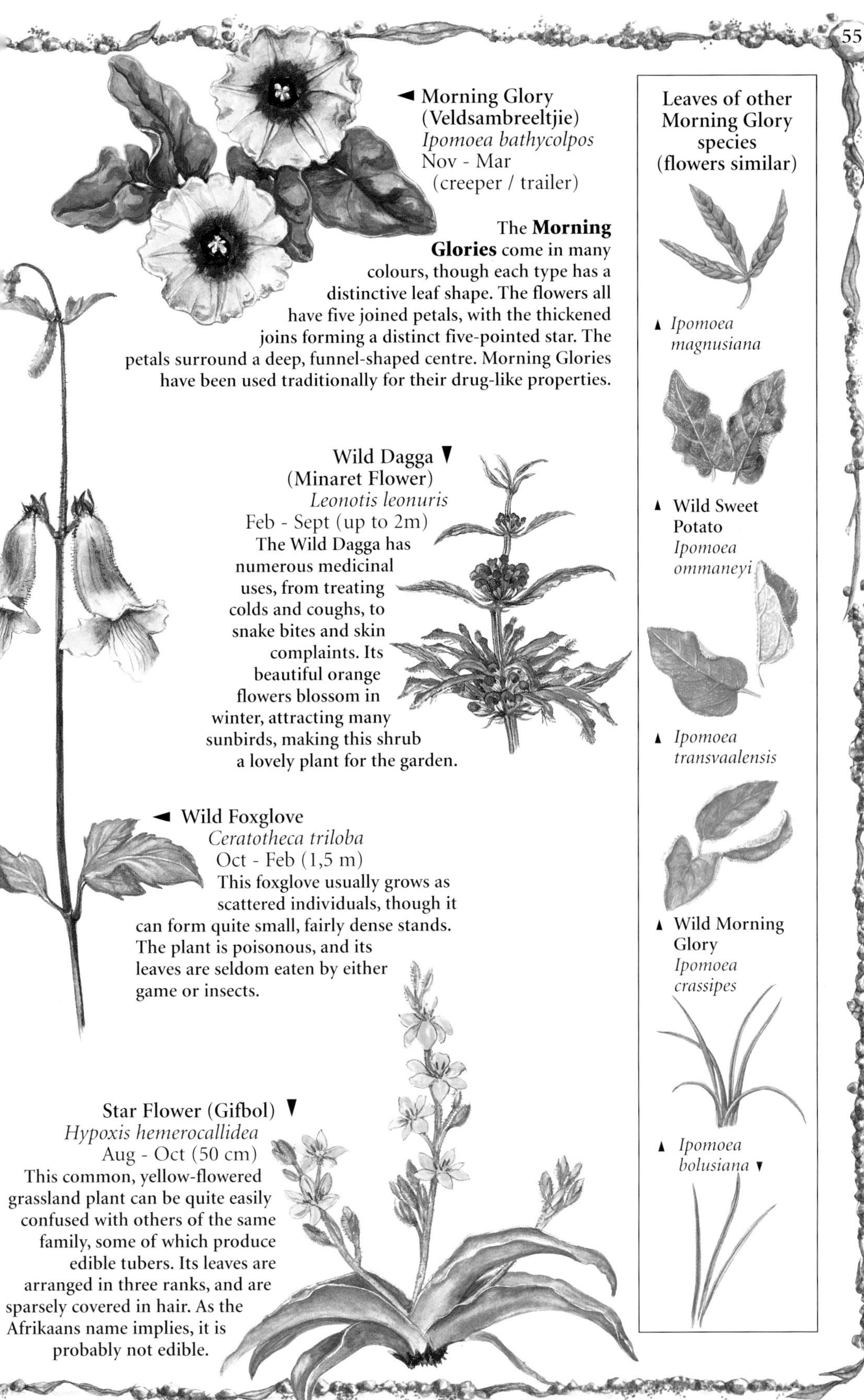

◄ Morning Glory (Veldsambreeltjie)
Ipomoea bathycolpos
Nov - Mar
(creeper / trailer)

The **Morning Glories** come in many colours, though each type has a distinctive leaf shape. The flowers all have five joined petals, with the thickened joins forming a distinct five-pointed star. The petals surround a deep, funnel-shaped centre. Morning Glories have been used traditionally for their drug-like properties.

Wild Dagga ▼
(Minaret Flower)
Leonotis leonuris
Feb - Sept (up to 2m)

The Wild Dagga has numerous medicinal uses, from treating colds and coughs, to snake bites and skin complaints. Its beautiful orange flowers blossom in winter, attracting many sunbirds, making this shrub a lovely plant for the garden.

◄ Wild Foxglove
Ceratotheca triloba
Oct - Feb (1,5 m)

This foxglove usually grows as scattered individuals, though it can form quite small, fairly dense stands. The plant is poisonous, and its leaves are seldom eaten by either game or insects.

Star Flower (Gifbol) ▼
Hypoxis hemerocallidea
Aug - Oct (50 cm)

This common, yellow-flowered grassland plant can be quite easily confused with others of the same family, some of which produce edible tubers. Its leaves are arranged in three ranks, and are sparsely covered in hair. As the Afrikaans name implies, it is probably not edible.

Leaves of other Morning Glory species (flowers similar)

▲ *Ipomoea magnusiana*

▲ Wild Sweet Potato
Ipomoea ommaneyi

▲ *Ipomoea transvaalensis*

▲ Wild Morning Glory
Ipomoea crassipes

▲ *Ipomoea bolusiana* ▼

Flowers

Relationships with Insects

Flowers are to insects and birds what helipads and airports are to aircraft. All good landing areas, whether plant or concrete, are clearly marked with landing instructions. Many flowers have ultra-violet patterns visible only to their specific insect pollinators, while night-time flowers are always light-coloured and easily seen.

Plants do not only attract insects that will pollinate them. They also provide shelter and food for insects that protect the plant from pests.

◄ Spotted Aloe
Aloe davyana (greatheadii)
May - Aug (90 cm)

During the winter, bees take pollen from this grass-loving aloe. The flower is very difficult to enter, and the bees become frustrated and very aggressive. The honey crop produced is reputedly one of the largest, from wild flowers, in the world.

African Honey Bee ►
Apis mellifera adansonii
(10 - 12 mm)

Aphid ▼
Family *Aphididae*
(1 - 2 mm)

Aphids are tiny insects that suck juices from plants, and then secrete a sweet nectar. This is enjoyed by certain ants which in return protect them from Ladybirds (shown here eating them). By injecting their own chemical cocktails into the plant, aphids communicate with one another and stimulate the plant to continue supplying food.

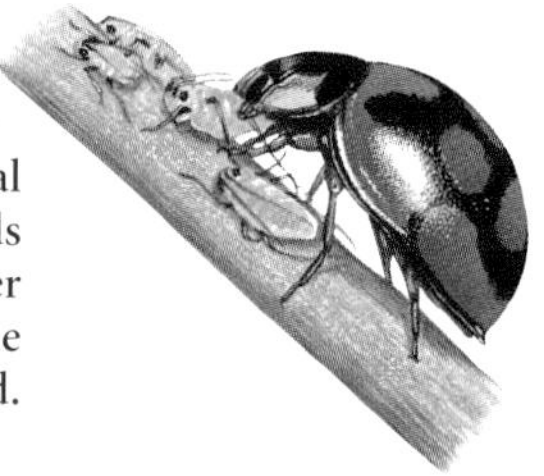

Warning colours of black-and-red and black-and-yellow identify insects that have either a bad taste or a very effective defence. The **African Honey Bee**, a most important pollinator, is well known for its sting. Black-and-red **Ladybirds** eat aphids, yet little preys on them.

◄ Ladybird
Family *Coccinellidae*
(5 - 7 mm)

◄ Lantana
Lantana camara
Nov - Jun (3 m)

These two species are **often found together.** **Lantana**, an alien from South America, is a highly troublesome weed forming dense, impenetrable thickets. The **Death's Head Hawk Moth** lays its eggs on this plant. The moth is unique in being able to utter squeaks, by blowing through its proboscis. The adult raids beehives, causing concern among beekeepers.

◄ Death's He
Hawk Mot
Acherontia
(50 mm)

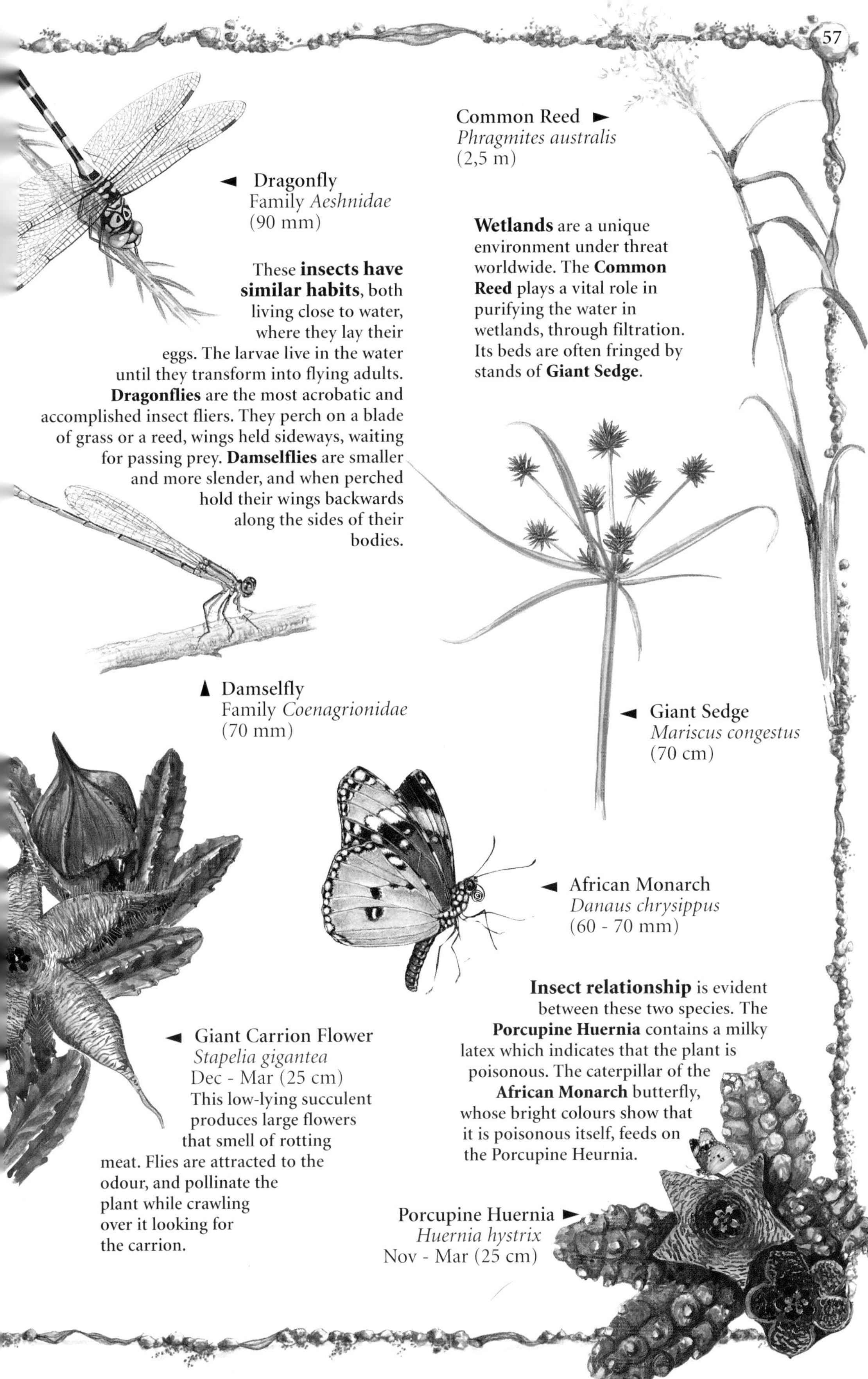

◄ Dragonfly
Family *Aeshnidae*
(90 mm)

These **insects have similar habits**, both living close to water, where they lay their eggs. The larvae live in the water until they transform into flying adults. **Dragonflies** are the most acrobatic and accomplished insect fliers. They perch on a blade of grass or a reed, wings held sideways, waiting for passing prey. **Damselflies** are smaller and more slender, and when perched hold their wings backwards along the sides of their bodies.

▲ Damselfly
Family *Coenagrionidae*
(70 mm)

Common Reed ►
Phragmites australis
(2,5 m)

Wetlands are a unique environment under threat worldwide. The **Common Reed** plays a vital role in purifying the water in wetlands, through filtration. Its beds are often fringed by stands of **Giant Sedge**.

◄ Giant Sedge
Mariscus congestus
(70 cm)

◄ African Monarch
Danaus chrysippus
(60 - 70 mm)

◄ Giant Carrion Flower
Stapelia gigantea
Dec - Mar (25 cm)
This low-lying succulent produces large flowers that smell of rotting meat. Flies are attracted to the odour, and pollinate the plant while crawling over it looking for the carrion.

Insect relationship is evident between these two species. The **Porcupine Huernia** contains a milky latex which indicates that the plant is poisonous. The caterpillar of the **African Monarch** butterfly, whose bright colours show that it is poisonous itself, feeds on the Porcupine Heurnia.

Porcupine Huernia ►
Huernia hystrix
Nov - Mar (25 cm)

Trees

Unique and Striking

Recognising the plants on this page is relatively easy. Each has an illustrated obvious feature that is unique to it. Many of these features are either associated with the plant's defence system, or used to attract the birds, insects or animals that pollinate it.

Trees reproduce themselves by means of colourful fruit and flowers that attract insects and birds. Do not pick the fruit and flowers wastefully. Leave them to serve the purpose for which they were intended.

▼ Cross-berry Raisin ► (Cross-berry)

Grewia occidentalis

(2 - 5 m) 463

The small, pinky-mauve flowers and the four-lobed fruit make this tree easy to spot. It likes sheltered, well-watered locations along streams, among rocks and on the edge of wooded areas. The wood makes excellent bows and spear shafts, and the softened, soaked bark can be used to dress wounds. The bark, used as shampoo, is believed to prevent hair from greying.

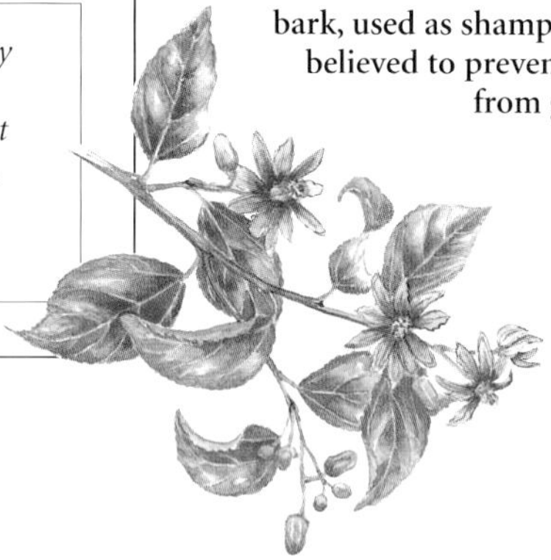

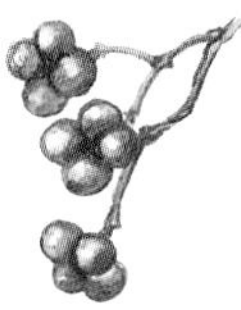

◄ Marula ▼

Sclerocarya birrea

(7 - 12 m) 360

The Marula is one of the more famous of Africa's trees, and has been protected and revered by humans for tens of thousands of years. Its fruit and leaves are eaten by many animals, birds and insects. Because of the high Vitamin C and sugar content, the fruit has innumerable food and medicine uses.

Stamvrug Milkplum ▼ ► (Transvaal Milkplum)

Englerophytum magalismontanum

(2 - 5 m) 581

Like the Marula the Milkplum contains plenty of Vitamin C, and is used to make wine, brandy, jelly and syrup. Many animals eat the fruit, and its tough wood is widely used for building.

▲ Olive Sagewood ►
(False Olive)
Buddleja saligna
(3 m) 636

The Olive Sagewood is common in groups along streams and singly on rocky slopes. Its wood was used for spear shafts. Today it is an important source of nectar for bee farmers.

◄ Highveld Cabbage-tree ▲
(Mountain Cabbage Tree)
Cussonia paniculata
(4 - 6 m) 563

Whether in grasslands or on slopes, this tree always grows among rocks which give it protection. In addition the corky bark makes it fire resistant. The wood was used for brake blocks on wagon wheels.

Mountain Aloe ►
Aloe marlothii
(2 - 5 m) 29.5

Kudu and eland browse the leaves of this very bitter plant, and humans also use it to control internal parasites. During the flowering season birds, monkeys and baboons feed on its abundant nectar.

Trees

Traditionally used Trees

Plants use complex chemical processes to convert sunlight into food. As they do this, different plant types produce different chemicals to help them remain healthy and productive. Humans have used this bountiful source of natural medicines for hundreds of thousands of years.

It is inadvisable to eat or suck any part of an unknown plant. What you see baboons or monkeys eat is not necessarily safe for humans.

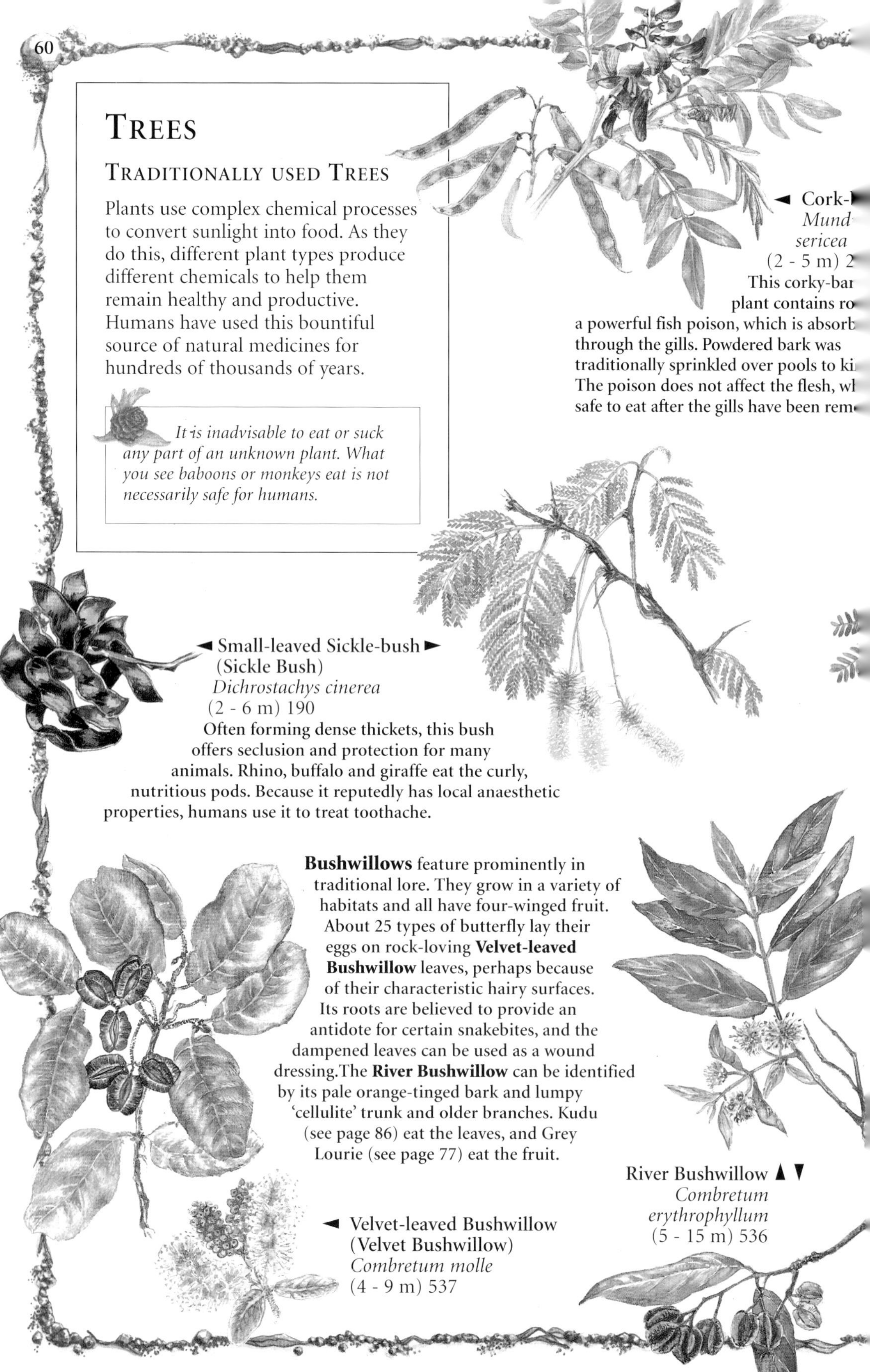

◄ Cork-
Mund
sericea
(2 - 5 m) 2
This corky-bar
plant contains ro
a powerful fish poison, which is absorb
through the gills. Powdered bark was
traditionally sprinkled over pools to ki
The poison does not affect the flesh, wh
safe to eat after the gills have been rem

◄ Small-leaved Sickle-bush ►
(Sickle Bush)
Dichrostachys cinerea
(2 - 6 m) 190

Often forming dense thickets, this bush offers seclusion and protection for many animals. Rhino, buffalo and giraffe eat the curly, nutritious pods. Because it reputedly has local anaesthetic properties, humans use it to treat toothache.

Bushwillows feature prominently in traditional lore. They grow in a variety of habitats and all have four-winged fruit. About 25 types of butterfly lay their eggs on rock-loving **Velvet-leaved Bushwillow** leaves, perhaps because of their characteristic hairy surfaces. Its roots are believed to provide an antidote for certain snakebites, and the dampened leaves can be used as a wound dressing. The **River Bushwillow** can be identified by its pale orange-tinged bark and lumpy 'cellulite' trunk and older branches. Kudu (see page 86) eat the leaves, and Grey Lourie (see page 77) eat the fruit.

River Bushwillow ▲ ▼
Combretum erythrophyllum
(5 - 15 m) 536

◄ Velvet-leaved Bushwillow
(Velvet Bushwillow)
Combretum molle
(4 - 9 m) 537

◄ Umbrella Acacia ►
(Umbrella Acacia)
Acacia tortilis
(3 - 6 m) 188

Thorn-tree Acacias in Africa all have compound, feathery leaves, and hooked or straight thorns. Hook-thorned Acacias, like the **Umbrella Acacia** and **Common Hook-thorn**, have long bottlebrush-like flowers. The straight-thorned variety, like the **Sweet-thorn Acacia** and **Broad-pod Splendid Acacia**, produce little pompom-like flowers. Many are important sources of traditional medicine remedies, for ailments ranging from headaches to bronchial and intestinal disorders. Their practical woods have been used for hundreds of implements and utensils, fence posts, and wagon parts including wheel bearings. Many animals browse the leaves, while bushbabies (see page 92) eat the gum.

◄ ▲ Broad-pod Splendid Acacia (Brack Thorn)
Acacia robusta robusta
(8 - 12 m) 183

Sweet-thorn Acacia ▲ ►
(Sweet Thorn)
Acacia karroo
(4 - 10 m) 172

◄ Common Hook-thorn Acacia
Acacia caffra
(5 - 10 m) 162

Trees

Rocks and Grassland

Grass is one of the more common plant types on Earth. Grass, like all other plants, converts Sun energy into plant material. This in turn provides food for a wide variety of grazing animals. Grasslands used to cover large areas, where the rainfall is about 600 mm per year, and where there is seasonal snow or frost. Throughout Africa many grasslands are maintained by regular fires that inhibit tree growth. Many of these plains are now used for agriculture.

Different grasses growing on a plain indicate different soils and drainage patterns. It is fun to be aware of these changing patterns, and of the animal populations they support.

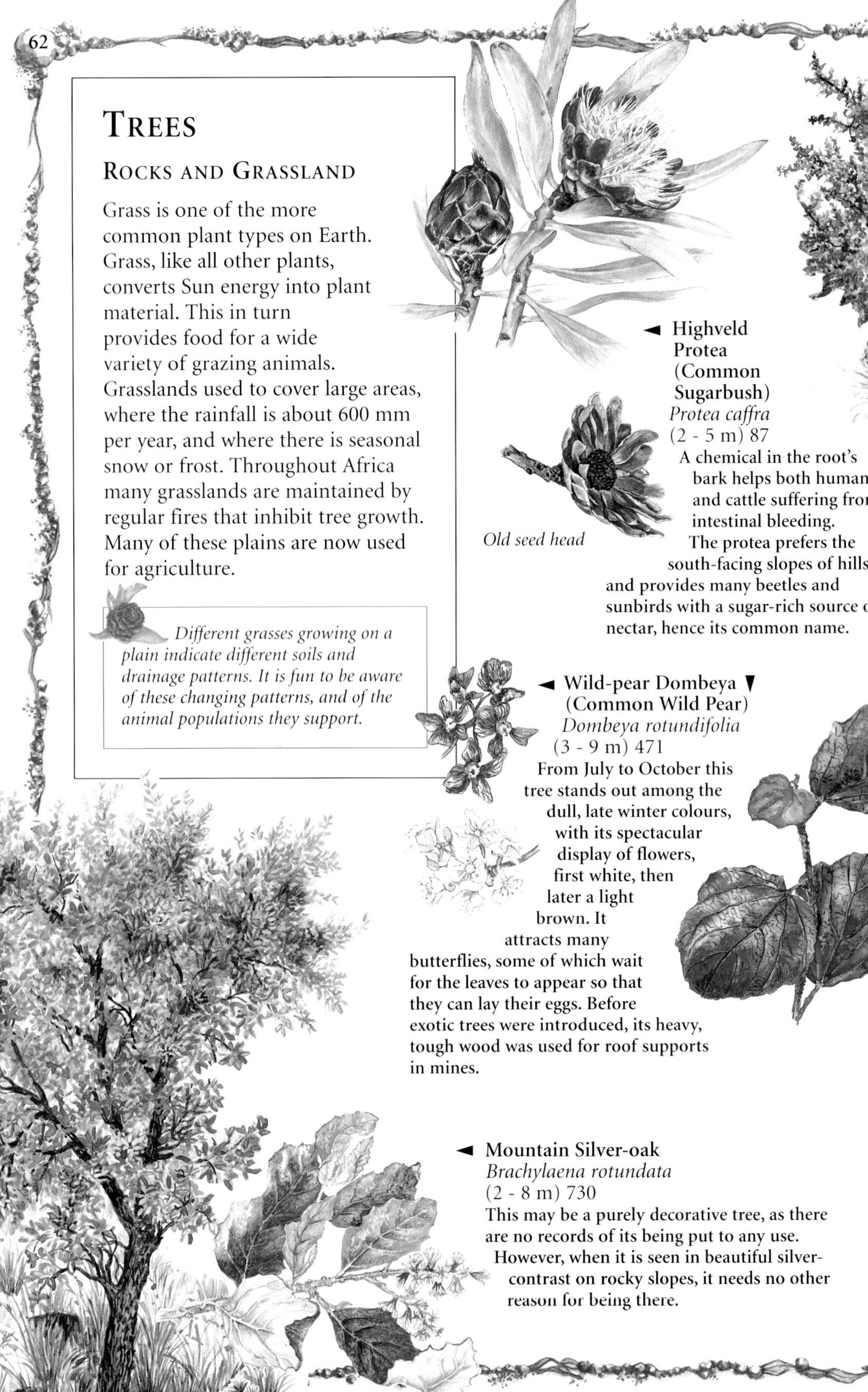

◄ **Highveld Protea (Common Sugarbush)**
Protea caffra
(2 - 5 m) 87

Old seed head

A chemical in the root's bark helps both humans and cattle suffering from intestinal bleeding. The protea prefers the south-facing slopes of hills, and provides many beetles and sunbirds with a sugar-rich source of nectar, hence its common name.

◄ **Wild-pear Dombeya** ▼ **(Common Wild Pear)**
Dombeya rotundifolia
(3 - 9 m) 471

From July to October this tree stands out among the dull, late winter colours, with its spectacular display of flowers, first white, then later a light brown. It attracts many butterflies, some of which wait for the leaves to appear so that they can lay their eggs. Before exotic trees were introduced, its heavy, tough wood was used for roof supports in mines.

◄ **Mountain Silver-oak**
Brachylaena rotundata
(2 - 8 m) 730

This may be a purely decorative tree, as there are no records of its being put to any use. However, when it is seen in beautiful silver-contrast on rocky slopes, it needs no other reason for being there.

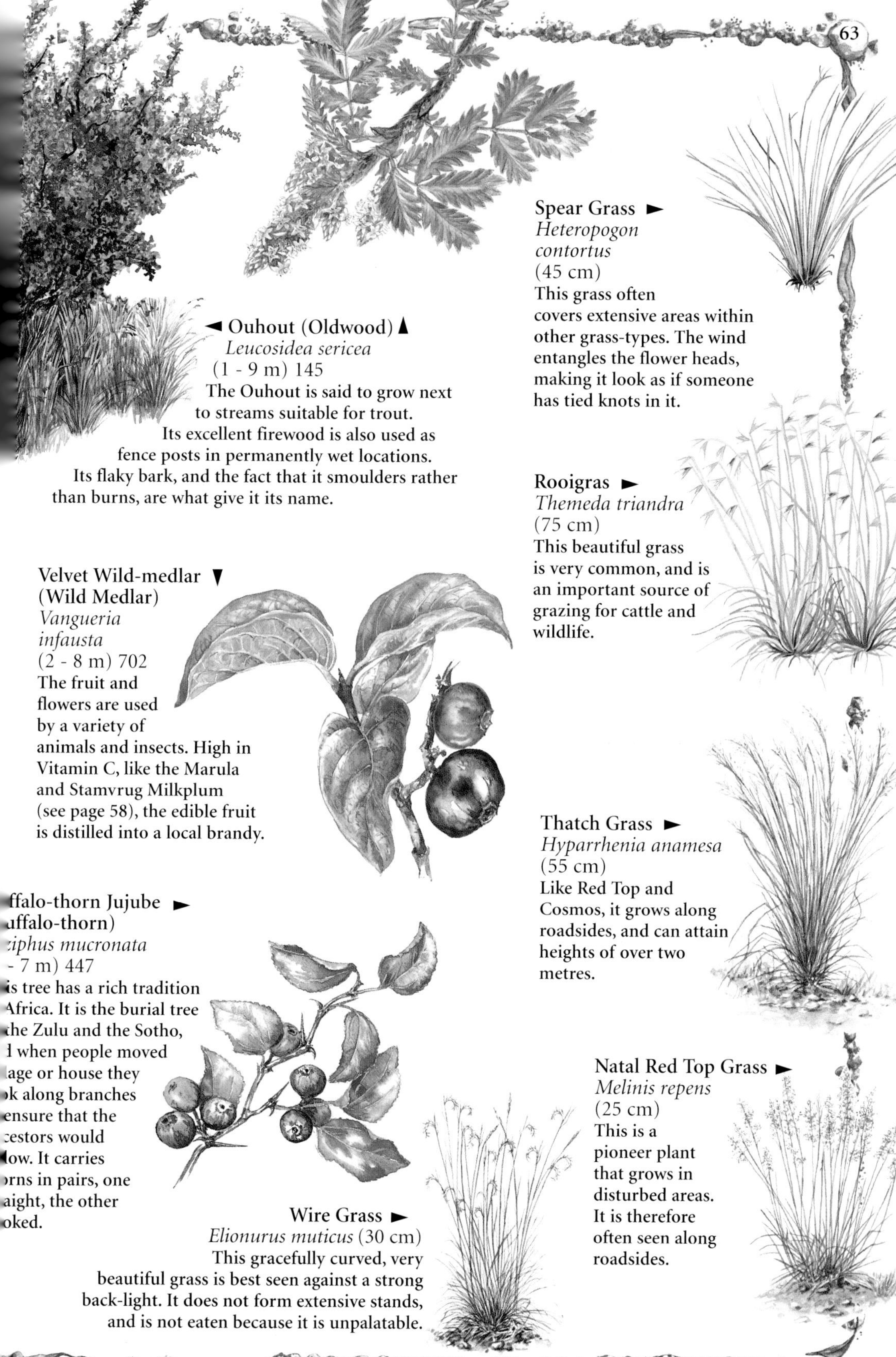

◄ Ouhout (Oldwood) ▲
Leucosidea sericea
(1 - 9 m) 145
The Ouhout is said to grow next to streams suitable for trout. Its excellent firewood is also used as fence posts in permanently wet locations. Its flaky bark, and the fact that it smoulders rather than burns, are what give it its name.

Spear Grass ►
Heteropogon contortus
(45 cm)
This grass often covers extensive areas within other grass-types. The wind entangles the flower heads, making it look as if someone has tied knots in it.

Rooigras ►
Themeda triandra
(75 cm)
This beautiful grass is very common, and is an important source of grazing for cattle and wildlife.

Velvet Wild-medlar ▼
(Wild Medlar)
Vangueria infausta
(2 - 8 m) 702
The fruit and flowers are used by a variety of animals and insects. High in Vitamin C, like the Marula and Stamvrug Milkplum (see page 58), the edible fruit is distilled into a local brandy.

Thatch Grass ►
Hyparrhenia anamesa
(55 cm)
Like Red Top and Cosmos, it grows along roadsides, and can attain heights of over two metres.

ffalo-thorn Jujube ►
uffalo-thorn)
ziphus mucronata
- 7 m) 447
is tree has a rich tradition Africa. It is the burial tree the Zulu and the Sotho, l when people moved age or house they ok along branches ensure that the cestors would low. It carries orns in pairs, one aight, the other oked.

Natal Red Top Grass ►
Melinis repens
(25 cm)
This is a pioneer plant that grows in disturbed areas. It is therefore often seen along roadsides.

Wire Grass ►
Elionurus muticus (30 cm)
This gracefully curved, very beautiful grass is best seen against a strong back-light. It does not form extensive stands, and is not eaten because it is unpalatable.

Trees

Open, Rocky Slopes

Open, but rocky, areas and slopes offer pockets of sheltered soil. The trees are hardy because there is little shelter from the hot sun of summer, or the cold winds, and maybe frosts, of winter. However these trees often grow in groups and shelter one another.

During thunderstorms it is unwise to take shelter among rocks or trees, as lightning strikes more frequently in their vicinity.

◄ Jacket-plum ▼
Pappea capensis
(4 - 10 m) 433
Jacket-plum fruit is eaten by t Black-collared Barbet (see page 76). Humans use it to mak vinegar and a tasty jelly and a multi-purpose o can be extracted from seed.

▲ Rose Beetle
(Fruit Chafer)
Family
Scarabaeidae
(20 - 25 mm)

Beetle types are more numerous than all other insect types in the world combined. Each has adapted to a special way of life. Towards the end of summer, when fruit is slowly rotting on or beneath trees, the **Rose Beetle** is often found half-buried in the feast. Its colouring (see Warning Colours page 56) indicates either that it has an unpleasant taste, or that a painful experience is in store for a would-be attacker. The **Dung Beetle** collects a ball of fresh dun which it buries after laying an egg in it. When the larva hatche it has a plentiful supply of food.

Dung Beetle ►
Family*Scarabaeidae*
(8 - 40 mm)

◄ African Olive ►
(Wild Olive)
Olea europaea
(2 - 10 m) 617
Pigeons, starlings and humans eat this fruit, and game and cattle eat the leaves. The wood makes beautiful furniture, and the leaves, a tasty tea. The fruit can be made into a very serviceable ink.

◄ **Common Spikethorn** ►
Gymnosporia buxifolia
(2 - 5 m) 399

The trunk and branches are not thick enough to provide useful furniture planks, so the wood is used for staves and utensils. The flowers have a strong, rather unpleasant smell, but Cape White-eyes (see page 78) eat the fruit.

▼ **Wild-peach**
Kiggelaria africana (4 - 12 m) 494

Flies pollinate this tree, but it also attracts butterflies, and consequently cuckoos. In autumn the fruit splits into four segments revealing its beautiful fleshy, orange interior. The wood turns water pink, and can be used as a dye.

Millipede (Songololo) ▼
Class *Diplopoda* (90 - 120 mm)

Millipedes (thousand-legs) are vegetarian. They move slowly, and readily curl themselves into a tight protective spiral.

Dwarf Sedge ►
Cyperus rupestris
(20 cm)

Unlike the Giant Sedge (see page 57), which thrives in wetlands, this much smaller sedge is found in poor, shallow soil, often among rocks.

▼ **Centipede**
Class *Chilopoda* (50 - 70 mm)

Centipedes (hundred legs) are poisonous, and are fast, active hunters of insects and worms. For humans their bite is about as painful as a bee sting.

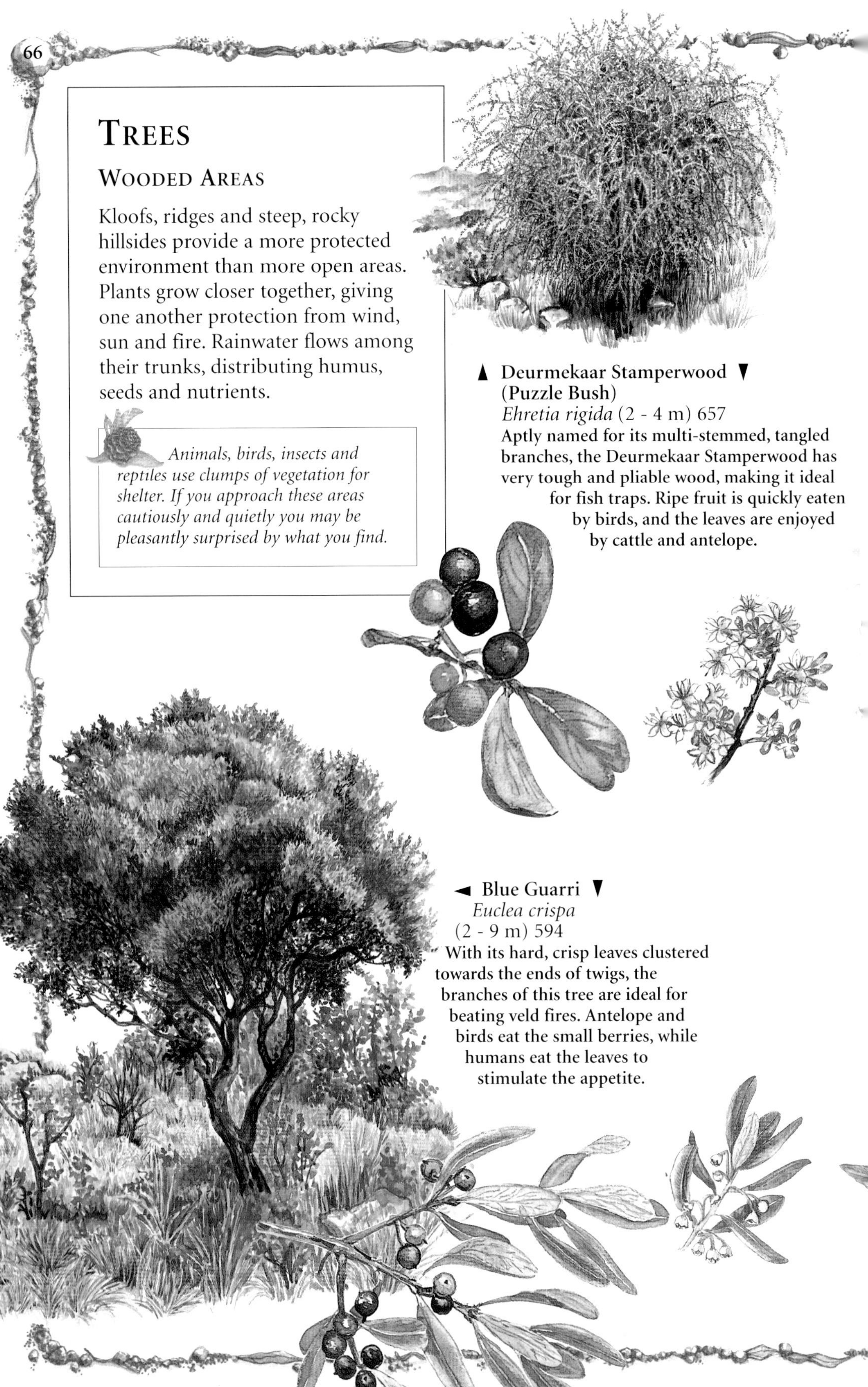

Trees

Wooded Areas

Kloofs, ridges and steep, rocky hillsides provide a more protected environment than more open areas. Plants grow closer together, giving one another protection from wind, sun and fire. Rainwater flows among their trunks, distributing humus, seeds and nutrients.

Animals, birds, insects and reptiles use clumps of vegetation for shelter. If you approach these areas cautiously and quietly you may be pleasantly surprised by what you find.

▲ **Deurmekaar Stamperwood** ▼
(Puzzle Bush)
Ehretia rigida (2 - 4 m) 657
Aptly named for its multi-stemmed, tangled branches, the Deurmekaar Stamperwood has very tough and pliable wood, making it ideal for fish traps. Ripe fruit is quickly eaten by birds, and the leaves are enjoyed by cattle and antelope.

◄ **Blue Guarri** ▼
Euclea crispa
(2 - 9 m) 594
With its hard, crisp leaves clustered towards the ends of twigs, the branches of this tree are ideal for beating veld fires. Antelope and birds eat the small berries, while humans eat the leaves to stimulate the appetite.

◄ **Inland Bladder-nut**
Diospyros whyteana
(2 - 10 m) 611

The Bladder-nut grows in rocky areas and ravines. Here it is often found in deep shade, with its shiny leaves standing out amongst the other vegetation. Its wood has been used for implement handles. It has an intriguing reputation as a remedy for impotency and infertility.

Bluebush Star-apple ▼
(Karoo Bluebush)
Diospyros lycioides
(2 - 7 m) 605

The Star-apple is shrub-like, has dull, hairy leaves, and is found in open grasslands. The roots blunt the toughest plough blade, while a chewed and frayed twig provides a fine toothbrush.

◄ Common Currant-rhus (Common Wild Currant)
Rhus pyroides
(2 - 9 m) 392

y Karee-rhus ▼
ntain Karree)

lictya
m) 387

All the **Rhus family** have groups of three leaves at the end of each leaf-stalk. Rhus leaves vary, not only from type to type, but also on a single tree. Some Rhus have thorns, like the **Common Currant-rhus**, which often grows on termite mounds, together with the Sweet-thorn Acacia (see page 61). The **Karee** has long, dark green, hard leaves, while the **Rocky Karee-rhus** has a softer, lighter green leaf.

Karee ►
Rhus lancea
(4 - 9 m) 386

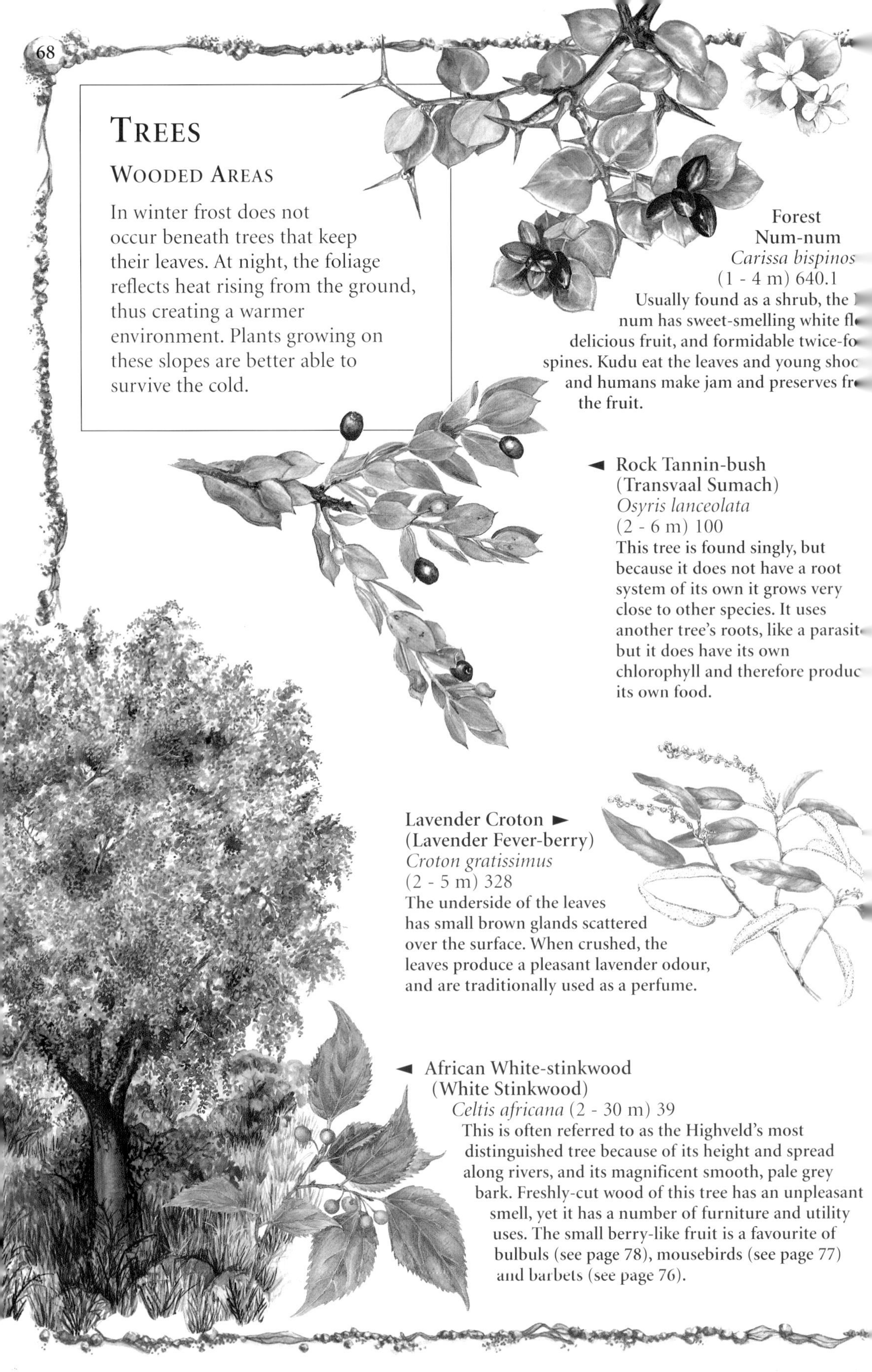

Trees

Wooded Areas

In winter frost does not occur beneath trees that keep their leaves. At night, the foliage reflects heat rising from the ground, thus creating a warmer environment. Plants growing on these slopes are better able to survive the cold.

Forest Num-num
Carissa bispinos
(1 - 4 m) 640.1
Usually found as a shrub, the num has sweet-smelling white fl delicious fruit, and formidable twice-fo spines. Kudu eat the leaves and young shoc and humans make jam and preserves fr the fruit.

◄ Rock Tannin-bush
(Transvaal Sumach)
Osyris lanceolata
(2 - 6 m) 100
This tree is found singly, but because it does not have a root system of its own it grows very close to other species. It uses another tree's roots, like a parasit but it does have its own chlorophyll and therefore produc its own food.

Lavender Croton ►
(Lavender Fever-berry)
Croton gratissimus
(2 - 5 m) 328
The underside of the leaves has small brown glands scattered over the surface. When crushed, the leaves produce a pleasant lavender odour, and are traditionally used as a perfume.

◄ African White-stinkwood
(White Stinkwood)
Celtis africana (2 - 30 m) 39
This is often referred to as the Highveld's most distinguished tree because of its height and spread along rivers, and its magnificent smooth, pale grey bark. Freshly-cut wood of this tree has an unpleasant smell, yet it has a number of furniture and utility uses. The small berry-like fruit is a favourite of bulbuls (see page 78), mousebirds (see page 77) and barbets (see page 76).

Many **insects use their wings to produce sound**. The flightless **King Cricket** produces sounds by rubbing its body plates together. Most **crickets** rub their wings softly against their legs to produce their night-time chirping sounds. Only female **mosquitoes** bite and produce a whine with their wings. They lay their eggs in still water. **Cicadas** also use their wings to produce a loud, very high-pitched, penetrating, continuous whine. Found among trees, they contribute characteristically to Africa's oppressive, singing daytime heat.

Cricket ▲
ktown Prawn)
ily *Stenopelmatidae*
55 mm)

Cricket ►
Family *Grillidae*
(15 - 35 mm)

Culex Mosquito ▲
Culex quinquefasciata
(7 - 9 mm)

Cicada ►
Family *Cicadidae*
(40 - 50 mm)

man-made forests of annesburg and Pretoria become ser and more luxuriant each year. nted in the suburbs for show, for uty and for privacy, the **Oak** and **aranda** have rewarded us with quiet nues, green vistas, peaceful roundings, beautiful flowers and an ctive pollution filter. Johannesburg is v known as the largest man-made est on Earth, and Pretoria is often led Jacaranda City. These forests have racted many bird and animal odland-species, that now find both d and shelter in the urban greenery. e whole area has become a delight for d watchers, especially in the warm mmers.

Oak ▲
Quercus robur
(15 - 30 m)
These large, stately trees, originally from England, provide dense, peaceful shade. They have been successfully planted along many older suburban roads and in parks.

◄ Jacaranda
Jacaranda mimosifolia (4 - 22 m)
The Jacaranda was originally imported from South America for its shade and beautiful flowers. Now it is actively invading surrounding areas along kloofs and river courses (see Problematic Alien trees, page 70).

Trees

Problematic and Alien

Plants that do not occur naturally in an area are called "exotics", and these can become "invasive aliens". Because they are from foreign places, exotics seldom have natural enemies in this country. They can become problematic invasive aliens when conditions and circumstances are so favourable that they start to propogate themselves spontaneously, without being planted by humans. They then begin to replace indigenous plants. Not all exotics become invasive aliens. In many well-planned forests the species chosen are easier to harvest. This controlled timber farming provides us with resources that in fact conserve our indigenous species. However it is vital that invasive aliens are not allowed to spread out of controlled plantations.

Landowners and businesses can make a significant difference by eliminating non-commercial invading trees from their properties.

Eucalyptus species ▲
(15 - 55 m)
This Australian tree uses vast quantities of water, with the result that it seriously depletes our available water reserves. Because it grows straight and fast it is ideal for mine supports, and farmers have used it to establish wind-breaks.

◄ **Syringa**
Melia azedarach
(5 - 23 m)
The Syringa's berry-like seeds are spread along water courses, where it soon establishes dense stands. Local trees and smaller plants are unable to compete, and gradually disappear from river and stream banks. The Syringa was introduced from India and South-East Asia. It can be eliminated by ring-barking, after which it dies.

Black Wattle ►
Acacia mearnsii
(5 - 10 m)
Originally introduced from Australia for the leather-curing tannin in its bark, this tree has become extremely successful at replacing local plants, and changing the characteristics and natural mechanisms of large tracts of undeveloped Highveld, particulaly in what should be beautiful kloofs and rocky areas.

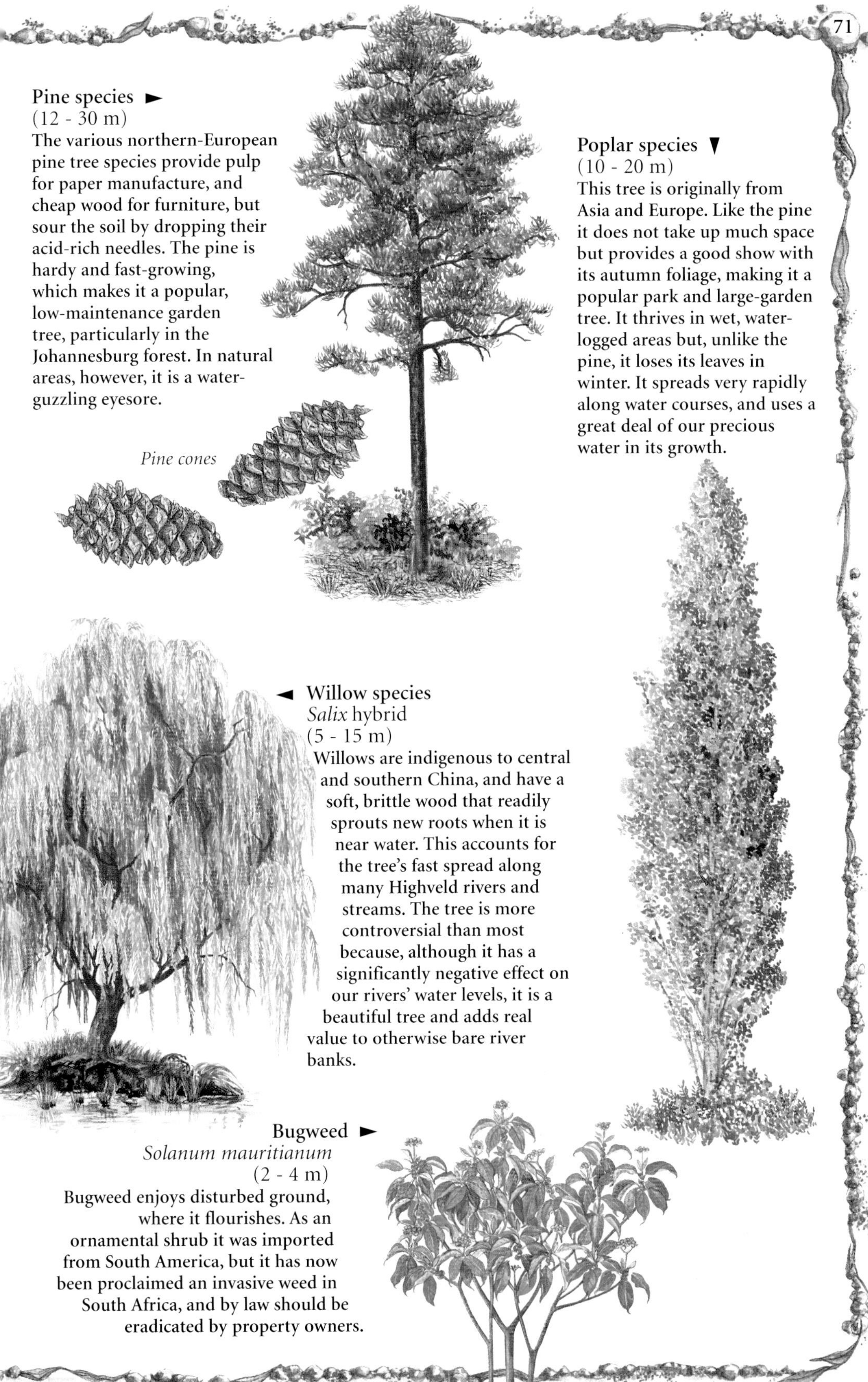

Pine species ►
(12 - 30 m)
The various northern-European pine tree species provide pulp for paper manufacture, and cheap wood for furniture, but sour the soil by dropping their acid-rich needles. The pine is hardy and fast-growing, which makes it a popular, low-maintenance garden tree, particularly in the Johannesburg forest. In natural areas, however, it is a water-guzzling eyesore.

Pine cones

Poplar species ▼
(10 - 20 m)
This tree is originally from Asia and Europe. Like the pine it does not take up much space but provides a good show with its autumn foliage, making it a popular park and large-garden tree. It thrives in wet, water-logged areas but, unlike the pine, it loses its leaves in winter. It spreads very rapidly along water courses, and uses a great deal of our precious water in its growth.

◄ Willow species
Salix hybrid
(5 - 15 m)
Willows are indigenous to central and southern China, and have a soft, brittle wood that readily sprouts new roots when it is near water. This accounts for the tree's fast spread along many Highveld rivers and streams. The tree is more controversial than most because, although it has a significantly negative effect on our rivers' water levels, it is a beautiful tree and adds real value to otherwise bare river banks.

Bugweed ►
Solanum mauritianum
(2 - 4 m)
Bugweed enjoys disturbed ground, where it flourishes. As an ornamental shrub it was imported from South America, but it has now been proclaimed an invasive weed in South Africa, and by law should be eradicated by property owners.

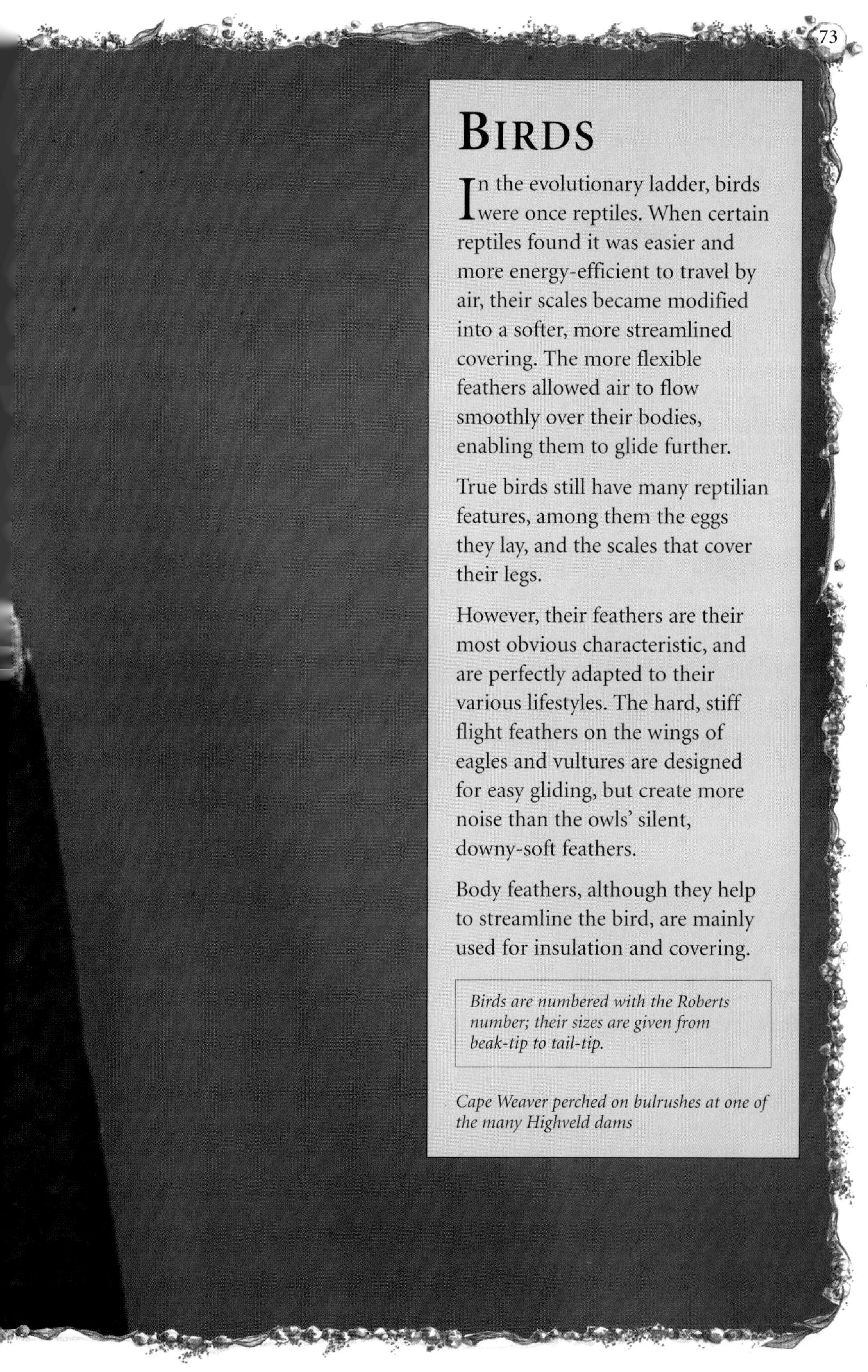

BIRDS

In the evolutionary ladder, birds were once reptiles. When certain reptiles found it was easier and more energy-efficient to travel by air, their scales became modified into a softer, more streamlined covering. The more flexible feathers allowed air to flow smoothly over their bodies, enabling them to glide further.

True birds still have many reptilian features, among them the eggs they lay, and the scales that cover their legs.

However, their feathers are their most obvious characteristic, and are perfectly adapted to their various lifestyles. The hard, stiff flight feathers on the wings of eagles and vultures are designed for easy gliding, but create more noise than the owls' silent, downy-soft feathers.

Body feathers, although they help to streamline the bird, are mainly used for insulation and covering.

Birds are numbered with the Roberts number; their sizes are given from beak-tip to tail-tip.

Cape Weaver perched on bulrushes at one of the many Highveld dams

Open Skies

Birds that spend much of their time in the air hunting for food have wings specifically designed for this lifestyle. The larger the bird's wings, the greater the lift. Therefore, eagles, vultures and kites have large, broad wings, which enable them to soar for long periods. The wing-tip feathers are separated, and look like fingers, which reduces turbulence over the wing. Swallows have narrow wings with a swept-back curved shape to ensure a fast, controlled and yet agile flight needed to hawk insects.

Birds have very specialised food needs. In today's rapidly expanding urban and industrial world, many of the habitats that provide food are disappearing. Think about whose dinner you may be picking, trampling, killing or driving over!

▲ Cape Vultur
Gyps coprotl
(1,1 m) 122

Scavengers keep the veld clean, and help prepare animal carcasses for quicker re-cycling. Among the first birds to arrive v be the **Cape Vulture**, capable if necessar ripping through the skin. When the carc fully opened, smaller birds like the **Pied Crow** will be dodging in and out to snatc what they can. The **Yellow-billed Kite**, a migrant from Europe, is often seen patrolling the roads, looking for anima killed by cars.

▼ Pied Crow
Corvus albus
(46 - 52 cm) 5

▲ Yellow-billed Kite
Milvus migrans parasitus
(55 cm) 126

◄ Hadeda Ibis
Bostrychia hagedash (76 cm) 94
The hadeda's call is a well-known sound of the bush. They call *'Ha ha...Hadeda'* when disturbed, or when leaving their roosts in the morning. They may be seen probing into the ground with their long, curved bills for earthworms.

◄ Lesser-striped Swallow ►
Hirundo abyssinica
(16 cm) 527

▼ White-rumped Swift ►
Apus caffer
(16 cm) 415

Swallows and **swifts** are often found together in groups. The **Lesser-striped Swallow** hawks its insect-prey in flight, and raises its brood in a cup-shaped mud nest attached to a rocky overhang or building. The fast-flying, insect-eating **White-rumped Swift** migrates throughout Africa. It uses swallow nests in South Africa during the breeding season (August and April).

▼ Black-shouldered Kite
Elanus caeruleus
(30 cm) 127

Steppe Buzzard
Buteo buteo
(45 - 50 cm) 149

Raptors spend their time watching for prey, either from prominent vantage points or while hovering and riding updrafts. **Steppe Buzzards** and **Black-shouldered Kites** feed on insects, rodents and small birds. The much larger **Black Eagle** hunts dassies (see page 92), and the occasional Vervet Monkey (see page 93), or small antelope.

▲ Striped Mouse
Rhabdomys pumilio
Rodent (Mammal)
(L incl tail: 18-21 cm)

◄ Black Eagle
Aquila verreauxii
(84 cm) 131

Bush and Trees

Three types of bird use this habitat. Some forage in the foliage, maintaining contact through the thick cover with songs and calls, and flashes of bright colour. Others use the sides and tops of the bushes and trees as perches, as they wait for their prey. Still other birds actually hide amongst the leaves and twigs, remaining still and camouflaged to avoid detection.

Do not leave thread, wool, or string lying about. Birds, looking for nesting material, may become entangled.

◄ Red-chested Cuckoo (Piet-my-vrou)
Cuculus solitarius (29 cm) 377
Like other cuckoos, this birds lays eggs in other birds' nests, leaving foster parents to raise the cuckoo chicks. Between October and Apri the three-note *'Piet-my-vrou'* call frequently heard. The bird itself is seldom seen, but may be heard anywhere from gardens to forests exotic plantations.

Cardinal Woodpecker ►
Dendropicos fuscescens
(15 cm) 486
While searching for caterpillars, this common woodpecker scurries around on dead trees, tapping the wood with its beak to open the beetles' tunnels. The sound of tapping on dry wood carries for long distances. Birds usually land low on the tree and work their way upwards.

Barbets have strong beaks, which they use to dig nesting holes in tree trunks or branches. They are highly vocal, with very characteristic calls. The **Crested Barbet** sounds like a bell-less alarm clock. It eats insects, and some fruit. The **Black-collared Barbet**, on the other hand, eats fruit and some insects. Its call is always a quickly-repeated duet. The male calls *'hoop'* first, immediately followed by the *'puh-duh-ly'* of the female.

Black-collared Barbet ►
Lybius torquatus
(20 cm) 464

▲ Crested Barbet
Trachyphonus vaillantii
(23 cm) 473

◄ Fiscal Shrike
Lanius collaris (21 - 23 cm) 732
Conspicuous in the garden and the wild, this bird sits on the highest and most prominent perches, usually on a dead twig, or on a tree or pole. Its black body is very boldly marked with a white front, and a white 'V' on the back. When food is plentiful, it stores it by impaling insects, small birds and lizards on thorns, or barbed-wire fencing.

◄ Spotted Eagle Owl
Bubo africanus
(47 cm) 401
Although it hunts at night, this owl is regularly seen during the day. It is a large bird, with pronounced ear-tufts and bright yellow eyes. Sometimes smaller birds mob it, and the commotion can help to reveal it, camouflaged, close to a tree trunk or against a rock.

▲ Masked Weaver
Ploceus velatus
(15 cm) 814
Named for its ability to weave its nest out of strands of grass, this weaver may be found both near water and in drier areas. Their remarkable enclosed nests hang from leaf-stripped, thin twigs, very often over water.

White-bellied Sunbird ►
Nectarinia talatala
(11 cm) 787
While the female is plain, the male White-bellied Sunbird has a brilliant green head. They are very active, feeding on insects and on nectar, which is sucked up with a tube-like tongue.

Red-faced Mousebird ►
Urocolius indicus
(34 cm) 426
Although smaller than the Grey Lourie this grey bird also looks like a little parrot. It has a crest and a parrot-shaped, fruit-eating beak. Instead of sitting upright on the perch, it appears to be falling off backwards.

◄ Grey Lourie
Corythaixoides concolor
(48 cm) 373
This large parrot-like bird is one of the characters of the bush, with its raucous '*go-away*' call. Because of urban trees and the availability of food, many more louries are now found in the cities.

In the Bush and on the Ground

Many birds are spotted on the ground first where they spend much of their time foraging for food (some of these birds are illustrated on the opposite page). They also, however, use the canopies of trees for nesting and shelter. Some birds may be seen perched on their favourite branch calling loudly. They are advertising their presence and territories, and may be trying to attract a mate.

Nest boxes and food trays will attract numerous birds to the garden. Planting indigenous trees in Gauteng is an even greater attraction, and will improve relationships between humans and the environment.

◄ White-fronted Bee-eater
Merops bullockoides
(23 cm) 443
Small groups of these very elegant birds perch with a clear all-round view, among trees or next to water. They wait for insects to fly past, then agilely hawk them in mid-air, returning to the perch to eat. They nest in 1-metre-long burrows excavated in river banks.

◄ Cape White-eye
Zosterops pallidus
(11 cm) 796
A common little bird that is usually heard before it is seen. Groups, foraging in dense growth for insects and sweet flower-parts, keep in touch through a continuous, soft twittering.

Glossy Starling ▲
Lamprotornis nitens (24 cm) 764
This bird is an optical delight. Bright sunlight makes it glisten dark, metallic green. To see the delightful subtleties of colour, however, watch it closely on a dull overcast day. It eats fruit, and can become very tame in gardens and at game park picnic sites.

◄ Black-eyed Bulbul
Pycnonotus barbatus
(22 cm) 568
The lovely liquid call is characteristic, uttered while foraging for fruit and insects. They are very useful birds, being quick to sound the alarm when a snake, cat, owl or mongoose is near. Like many other medium-sized birds, they have a *'chissik chissik'* warning call.

▼ Cape Robin ►
Cossypha caffra (16 - 18 cm) 601
This little bird hunts insects and spiders in thick undergrowth, or quickly retreats there when disturbed. It is most easily spotted, and identified, by the flash of its orange tail, and the smart white brow-strip. As it perches, it briefly fans its tail, giving a glimpse of colour.

Red-chested Cuckoo chick being fed by its Cape Robin foster mother

▼ Hoopoe
Upupa epops (26 cm) 451
The hoopoe eats mainly insect larvae and worms, which it finds in the ground by probing with its long beak. It erects a fan-shaped crest when alarmed, and flies as if its wings are too soft for its body weight. It says its name when calling *'hoop-hoop'*.

Cape Wagtail ▼
Motacilla capensis
(19 - 20 cm) 713
The wagtails characteristically ; their tails up and down when ıey walk. The Cape Wagtail is a mmon resident, and is en seen in suburbia, where it becomes very tame.

▼ Olive Thrush
Turdus olivaceus (24 cm) 577
Very common under garden shrubs and on lawns, the Olive Thrush is a useful snail hunter. In forests and dense bush it is more secretive, spending most of its time in the leaf litter. It feeds on insects, on fruit in season, and on the occasional lizard or nestling.

◄ Laughing Dove
Streptopelia senegalensis
(25 cm) 355
Most easily recognised by its pinky, spotted chest, it is a strong, direct flier, easily maintaining speeds faster than 65 km/hr. This is one of the commonest birds of the region. Males pursue females along the ground or branch with a comic hunched, hopping gait.

Grass and Rocks

Grasslands provide many habitats. The scattered rocks offer shelter and serve as lookout posts. Some birds probe and scratch in the soil and beneath the stones, while the seed-eaters cling to drooping grass stems, and the hunters stalk the expanses or patrol the skies.

Binoculars enable you to see the subtle and beautiful patterns on birds that, to the naked eye, appear to be drab.

(F)

(Breeding M)

◄ Long-tailed Widow ►
Euplectes progne
(Breeding 55 - 60 cm; non-breeding 20 - 22 cm) 832

During summer, these long-tailed birds are a common sight flying over the veld, or foraging for seeds and insects next to roads. All females, and non-breeding males, are a drab brown. Males display by holding their tails vertically downward in flight, but let them stream behind when simply flying from one place to another.

(Breeding M)

◄ Red Bishop
Euplectes orix
(11 - 13 cm) 824

In summer the males take on their bright red-and-black breeding plumage. In winter they resemble the drab-brown females and juveniles. Red Bishops nest in reed beds, and males display by puffing themselves up, and flying around on rapidly-beating wings. They are seed-eaters, and always gather in flocks.

Helmeted Guineafowl ▲
Numida meleagris
(53 - 58 cm) 203

Guineafowl always gather in groups as they scratch and peck around looking for seeds and grubs. They stay on the ground, relying on running before taking to flight.

Cape Sparrow ►
Passer melanurus
(14 - 16 cm) 803

These little birds are so common that they are often taken for granted. They gather in groups, and industriously hop around picking up seeds. At breeding time, which may be in any season, pairs build a large, very untidy mess of a nest, with any materials they can find.

(F)

(M)

Rock Pigeon ▼
Columba guinea
(33 cm) 349
…handsome birds may be seen leaving …ocky roosts in high-flying flocks …n the morning, or returning at …g. During the day they …singly or in pairs. …re very strong …covering …distances to …ed or grain.

Red-winged Starling ▼
Onychognathus morio
(27 - 28 cm) 769
Like the Rock Pigeon, this starling builds its nests on cliff ledges. Even when they gather in large groups, individuals keep in touch with a pleasant, liquid, whistle-like call. They feed on insects, fruit and aloe nectar, and have also been seen to remove ticks from antelope.

(F)

(M)

◄ Cattle Egret
Bubulcus ibis
(54 cm) 71
These birds are often found in large numbers, in association with grazing animals. They feed on the insects disturbed by the moving herd. They fly in large V-formations to and from their communal roosts in reed beds.

▼ Crowned Plover
Vanellus coronatus
(30 cm) 255
This plover, with its obvious crown, prefers sparsely-grassed or burnt areas. When feeding, it walks a few paces, sticks its tail in the air, and stares closely at the ground before pecking at an insect-morsel. Eggs are simply laid among loosely gathered stones. Adults defend their nests by dive-bombing intruders, including humans!

Long-legged birds like these hunt in different habitats. The **Secretary Bird** seldom stands still, but strides through the veld looking for insects, rodents and small reptiles. It is possibly named for the long 'quill pens' it keeps behind its 'ear'. The **Black-headed Heron** either stands and waits for its prey, fishing in slow-moving or stagnant water, or hunts in open grass, stalking rodents, frogs or reptiles.

…ry Bird ►
…gittarius
…entarius
…m) 118

◄ Black-headed Heron
Ardea melanocephala
(97 cm) 63

Water Birds

Birds that swim can be divided into two groups: those that habitually dive, and those that cannot. When taking flight the divers, like cormorants, always run across the surface before becoming airborne. Non-diving, dabbling birds, such as ducks, leap directly into the air. Exceptions to this rule are those surface-feeding birds that are just too large to leap into the air, such as flamingos and swans.

Water that becomes polluted by pleasure boats, sewerage, garbage or industrial effluent cannot provide either a comfortable home zone for birds, or a satisfying recreational adventure for you.

◄ Reed Cormorant
Phalacrocorax africanus
(60 cm) 58

These water birds **swim very low in the water**, and check for fish by ducking their heads below the surface. **Reed Cormorants** and **Darters** dive for fish and frogs, but because their feathers are not totally waterproof, they gradually become waterlogged. After swimming they can often be seen standing on low-lying rocks or stumps, holding their wings out to dry.

Darter ▲
Anhinga melanogaster
(79 cm) 60

Spur-winged Goose ▼
Plectropterus gambensis
(1 m) 116

▲ Yellow-billed D
Anas undu
(51 - 63 cm)

Ducks and geese **usually gather in large flocks**. If they are present in pairs, they are breeding. **Geese** often graze in grasslands or farmers' fields, and **ducks** dabble in shallow water or up-end where it is deeper. They have webbed feet, and flattened beaks with a filter comb around the inside edge, for straining particles of food and micro-organisms from water.

Egyptian Goose ►
Alopochen aegyptiacus
(63 - 73 cm) 102

(M)

(M)

▲ Pied Kingfisher
Ceryle rudis
(25 - 29 cm) 428

Kingfishers are ideally suited to diving for prey. They will wait patiently, then plunge, catch the prey and return to the perch to kill it. The **Giant** and **Pied Kingfishers** perch over water, waiting for a fish to swim within range. Favourite branches are often coated in fish scales. In drier areas, species like the **Brown-hooded Kingfisher** have an insect diet.

Kingfisher ▲
eryle maxima
-6 cm)

◄ Brown-hooded Kingfisher
Halcyon albiventris
(24 - 25 cm) 435

African Fish Eagle ►
Haliaeetus vocifer (63 - 73 cm) 148
This fine bird is usually first noticed as a white patch, high in a tree overlooking an expanse of water. Mates give their characteristic ringing call to each other from perches, or while circling high overhead. They snatch fish near the surface, eating larger ones on the ground, next to the water.

▼ Red-knobbed Coot
Fulica cristata (43 cm) 228
These very common birds can be seen on almost every stretch of inland water. They dabble or dive for plant food, but always bring it to the surface to eat. Breeding males often chase one another across the water, running on their partially webbed, over-sized feet.

Dabchick (Little Grebe) ►
Tachybaptus ruficollis (20 cm) 8
The small, round dabchick dives well, and can cover large distances under water, hunting for frogs and small fish. It often flaps its wings, raising itself high in the water, then settling back with a vigorous body-shake.

MAMMALS

Mammals represent the ultimate in embryo-care systems. Rather than entrusting their precious unborn to the dangers of an egg hidden in a hole, crevice or nest, the female keeps it within her body until it is born. Even then, the newborn is cared for in a very personal way, and fed directly from the mother's special mammary glands with food prepared within the mother's body. This system must surely offer developing embryos, and newborn babies, the ultimate in controlled environment, special protection and personalised feeding.

During a lengthy childhood, youngsters are taught the social and the physical lifestyles required of their type. Only after a significantly longer period than any fish, amphibian or reptile is privileged to have, do they venture out into an independent adult life of their own.

Mammals are measured in height H - ground to shoulder, or in length L - tip of nose to tip of tail.

Black-backed Jackal are frequently seen trotting through the veld, in a busy fashion.

Herbivores

All herbivores (grazers and browsers) have broad, flat, grinding back teeth to crush and mix the food with saliva. Certain animals, like rhino and zebra, have very large digestive tracts to process large quantities of food. Others (known as ruminants) have complex, four-chambered stomachs used for partially breaking down and storing the food. They can then return the food to their mouths, and re-chew it again to extract further nutrients (rumination).

Browsers

The type of habitat a herbivore is found in will give an indication of its feeding habits. Browsers are therefore mostly found in wooded areas. Many browsers will switch to grazing, depending on the season and quality of food available, to obtain enough nutrition. Eland mostly browse, but graze on fresh grass in summer to satisfy their high protein requirements.

If you are in a park, with one of the Big Five it is very dangerous and irresponsible to leave your vehicle!

(F)

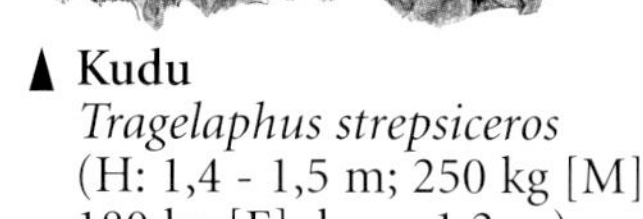

▲ Kudu
Tragelaphus strepsiceros
(H: 1,4 - 1,5 m; 250 kg [M], 180 kg [F]; horn 1,2 m)

Kudu and eland are two of the **largest antelope** found in South Africa, the eland being the largest, clearing two-metre fences with apparent ease. **Kudu** live in small groups in woodland savannah and hilly terrain. They are fairly shy and are always on the alert for disturbance, barking or running to the nearest cover when alarmed. **Eland** mostly live in small groups, but sometimes form large herds, across a wide range of habitats.

◄ Eland
Taurotragus oryx
(H: 1,6 m; 700 kg
450 kg [F]; horn 6

(F)

(M)

◄ Common Duiker
Sylvicapra grimmia
(H: 50 cm; 18 kg [M], 21 kg [F]; horn 11 cm)

The Common Duiker is widespread, living a solitary life except during breeding or when females move with their young. When threatened it lies low in the grass to hide, but when approached too closely will suddenly dart off in a zig-zag course, disappearing into the bush.

► Giraffe
Giraffa camelopardalis
(Total height: 3,9 - 5,2 m [M],
3,7 - 4,7 m [F];
970 - 1 400 kg [M],
700 - 950 kg [F])

These large animals both have **very tough tongues** and lips that protect them from the sharp thorns that some of their favourite food plants carry, like Acacias (see page 61). The **giraffe** is the tallest animal in the world, but still only has seven neck vertebrae (like humans). It lives in scrub and woodland habitats, while the **Black Rhino** prefers dense bush or thickets. The Black Rhino is slightly smaller and more aggressive than the White Rhino (see page 88).

▲ Black or Hook-lipped Rhinoceros
Diceros bicornis
(H: 1,6 - 2,0 m;
800 - 1 100 kg;
record horn 1,05 m)

(M)

Impala ▲
Aepyceros melampus
(H: 90 cm; 45 kg; horn 50 cm)

Elephant and impala **browse and graze depending on availability**. **Impala** live in small to large breeding and bachelor herds. At the start of the breeding season (April and May), the snorting and grunting of sparring males can be heard over great distances. **Elephants** live in stable, social units led by a matriarch. Mature bulls form bachelor groups or are seen wandering alone. Elephants communicate with one another over several kilometres using infrasonic sound, which is inaudible to the human ear.

◄ Elephant
Loxodonta africana
(H: 3,2 - 4,0 m [M],
2,5 - 3,4 m [F];
5 000 - 6 300 kg [M],
2 800 - 3 500 kg [F])

Herbivores

Grazers

Grazers and browsers are well adapted to the habitats in which they are found. Grazers are usually spotted in large groups on the open, grassy plains, while browsers (see pages 86, 87) are usually found in smaller groups in woodland habitats. Living in large groups provides greater protection against predators in open areas where there is little cover. While browsers have narrow muzzles to pick leaves and twigs off trees, grazers have broad, flattened mouths adapted for eating grass. This difference is distinctive in the Black Rhino (see page 87) and White Rhino, with a hook-lip and square-lip respectively to match their feeding habits.

Although they appear docile and calm, herbivores are formidably armed with horn, tusk and/or hoof. These are good reasons why predators and humans should never take them for granted.

◄ White or Square-l
Rhinoceros
Ceratotherium sin
(H: 1,8 m;
1 400 - 2 300 kg; r
horn 1,58 m)

The White Rhino and Hippopotamus are **large, grazers.** The **White Rhino** is found in open savannah in small groups, also preferring short g **Hippos** spend all day in the water, but at night n cover many kilometres feeding on short grass. Th are gregarious, with dominant bulls, living in her about 15. Both create large dung piles, w mark their presence – while the r scatters his dung with his back the hippo flaps his tail marking several metres of vegetation.

◄ Hippopotamus
Hippopotamus amphibius
(H: 1,5 m; 1 000 - 2 000 k
1 000 - 1 700 kg [F])

◄ Waterbuck ►
Kobus ellipsiprymnus
(H: 1,3 m; 250 - 270 kg;
horn 75 cm)

A white ring around the rump and lyre-shaped, forward-pointing horns, make this impressive antelope unmistakable. Waterbuck live in small herds close to water, and will swim readily to seek refuge from danger.

These are **gregarious animals that often graze together. Zebra** prefer taller grass, while **wildebeest** prefer short grass, and so often follow up behind the zebra. Wildebeest rely on the zebra's good eyesight and alertness. The zebra's stripes also confuse predators when the herd bunches up together appearing as one unit.

◄ Plains Zebra (Burchell's Zebra)
Equus quagga antiquorum
(H: 1,3 m; 290 - 340 kg)

Blue Wildebeest ►
Connochaetes taurinus
(H: 1,4 m; 180 - 250 kg; horn 60 cm)

Sable Antelope ▼
Hippotragus niger
(H: 1,35 m; 230 kg; horn 1 m)

These **striking antelope have formidable horns** and handsome coats. **Sable** live in herds of 10 - 30 animals in savannah woodlands, and are dependent on water. **Gemsbok** are also gregarious, but prefer open, arid areas, and are independent of water. Both use their horns to fight off predators.

d Hartebeest ►
elaphus buselaphus
: 1,25 m; 140 kg;
rn 52 cm)

e of the fastest antelope southern Africa, the hartebeest ily outruns most predators over istance. They are social animals, urring in a scattered herd of up 20 individuals. Both sexes carry rns.

Gemsbok ▲
Oryx gazella
(H: 1,2 m; 240 kg [M], 210 kg [F])

Carnivores

The carnivores that hunt living prey are equipped with excellent eyesight and hearing, sharp claws and teeth, and powerful, fleet bodies. Scavengers do not need this range of aggressive weaponry, but their sense of smell is acute. The teeth and jaws of the scavengers that eat bones are even more powerful than those of the active hunters.

Be aware of an animal's body language. Ears, tail, pupils, eyebrows, lips, breathing and general body posture all give clues to its feelings and intentions.

▲ **Leopard**
Panthera pardus
(H: 70 - 80 cm; 40 -

Hunters are usually at the top of the food chain, preying on herbivores or plant eater **Leopards**, still common in many areas quit close to large settlements, hunt at night by ambushing their prey, and prefer rocky areas where dassie (see page 92) and baboons (see page 93) live. **Cheetahs** live in open areas where they can attain speeds of about 100 km/hr. They are built for speed with long, thin bodies, flattened heads, and rudder-like tails. **Lions** need some concealment for stalking, and cover the final distance in a fast charge. Although the lionesses often do the hunting, the males feed first. The high mortality among lion cubs, due to starvation and to cuffing from feeding males, controls their numbers.

◄ **Cheetah**
Acinonyx jubatus
(H: 80 cm; 40 - 60 kg)

(M) *(F)*

◄ **Lion**
Panthera leo
(H: 1,2 m [M], 1,0 m [F];
150 - 225 kg [M], 110 - 152 kg

Slender Mongoose ▼
Galerella sanguinea
(L: 50 - 65 cm;
500 - 800 g [M],
370 - 560 g [F])

Small carnivores, like the solitary **Slender Mongoose**, are often seen along the roadside, hunting rodents, reptiles, birds and insects. By night, the **Small-spotted Genet**, an agile climber, spends most of its time hunting birds and insects.

Small-spotted Genet ►
Genetta genetta
(L: 0,8 - 1,0 m; 1,5 - 2,6 kg)

Cape Clawless Otter ▼
Aonyx capensis (L: 1,3 m; 13 kg)
This otter has no claws as the feet are used more for feeling and grasping. It inhabits salt and fresh water, where it hunts shellfish, crabs and fishes. A small pile of dung on the rocks (mostly made up of colourful crab and fish fragments) is often the first sign that an otter is about.

◄ Black-backed Jackal
Canis mesomelas
(H: 38 cm; 6 - 10 kg)

▼ Brown Hyaena
Hyaena brunnea
(H: 80 cm; 45 kg)

Scavengers are the ultimate feeding opportunists. They sometimes hunt and kill animals, but actively seek carcasses left by farmers or hunting carnivores. Both **jackals** and **hyaenas** successfully steal meat while larger carnivores are actually feeding. All the while, other species like the Pied Crow (see page 74), vultures (see page 74), and even insects, will be darting in and out grabbing what they can. The powerful-jawed hyaena demolishes the bones. In this way nothing is wasted.

Other Mammals

Small animals generally require a smaller area than large animals to find sufficient food. Once you have found a smaller animal, the chances are quite good that the species will be in the same general vicinity regularly. Larger mammals have to cover long distances when hunting, and are therefore not as predictable in their location.

Despite their cuteness, do not try to play with or feed any wild animal. They quickly become adventurous, aggressive and dangerous, and worst of all dependent on human hand-outs.

◄ **Lesser Bushbaby**
Galago moholi
(L: 30 - 40 cm; 150 g)
These large-eyed, nocturnal, tree-dwelli animals are capable of leaping up to 10 r from one branch to another. Their eyes, positioned in the front of the head, enable to judge distance and landing site perfectly. Tl main diet is gum from Acacias (see page 61), bu also catch insects.

▲ **Porcupine**
Hystrix africaeaustralis
(L: 0,75 - 1,0 m; 10 - 24 kg)
The porcupine is southern Africa's largest rodent. all rodents, porcupines must continually gnaw thi to keep their teeth the correct length. The teeth not worn away, would grow nearly 10 cm per The impressive spines are hollow, quite loose attached, modified hairs that are used to det predators.

▲ **Warthog**
Phacochoerus aethiopicus
(H: 70 cm; 60 - 150 kg)
Warthogs, named after their facial warts, have more character and personality than many other species. If undisturbed, they will approach quite close, busily rooting about on their knees. When disturbed, they first spend a few seconds staring, then run off with tails held stiffly aloft.

▼ **Dassie (Rock Hyrax)** ▲
Procavia capensis
(L: 45 - 60 cm; 2,5 - 4,6 kg)
The dassie has a poorly-developed ability to control its own body temperature, and during the cool, earl morning hours will often be found sitting on the warming rock faces, much as reptiles do. They are eaten by large bird of prey, especially the Black Eagle (see page 75). Such birds often attack with the sun behind them, so hyraxes have evolved a sunshade within the eye, and are able to look almost directly into the sun. Interestingly, their closest relative is another browser/grazer, the elephant.

Cape Serotine Bat ►
Eptesicus capensis
(L: 8,5 cm; wingspan 24 cm; 6,5 g)
Bats are the only mammals capable of true flight. This bat will be seen after dusk, swooping and twisting after insects, well above tree height. Insect-eating bats use echolocation to find their prey at night. They emit high-pitched squeaks, and listen to the echoes that bounce back.

◄ Vervet Monkey ►
Cercopithecus aethiops
(L: 1,0 - 1,3 m [M], 0,95 - 1,1 m [F]; 5,5 kg [M], 4,0 kg [F])
Vervets, more common than baboons, are also social and omnivorous. However, they spend their time in the trees near rivers, using them for food, shelter and refuge. They signal both fear and aggression by raising their eyebrows, revealing light skin that contrasts strongly with the black face.

Chacma Baboon ►
Papio ursinus
(L: 1,2 - 1,6 m [M], 1,0 - 1,2 m [F]; 32 kg [M], 16 kg [F])
Baboons are ground-based but sleep, find efuge and post sentries in trees. They live in organised social troops, and range across a iety of more open environments. They are nivorous, and band together to defend the troop. Even their arch-enemy, the leopard e page 90), usually waits until after k before attacking. Baboons a real pest and threat in farming communities, nd despite being constantly hunted are very successful.

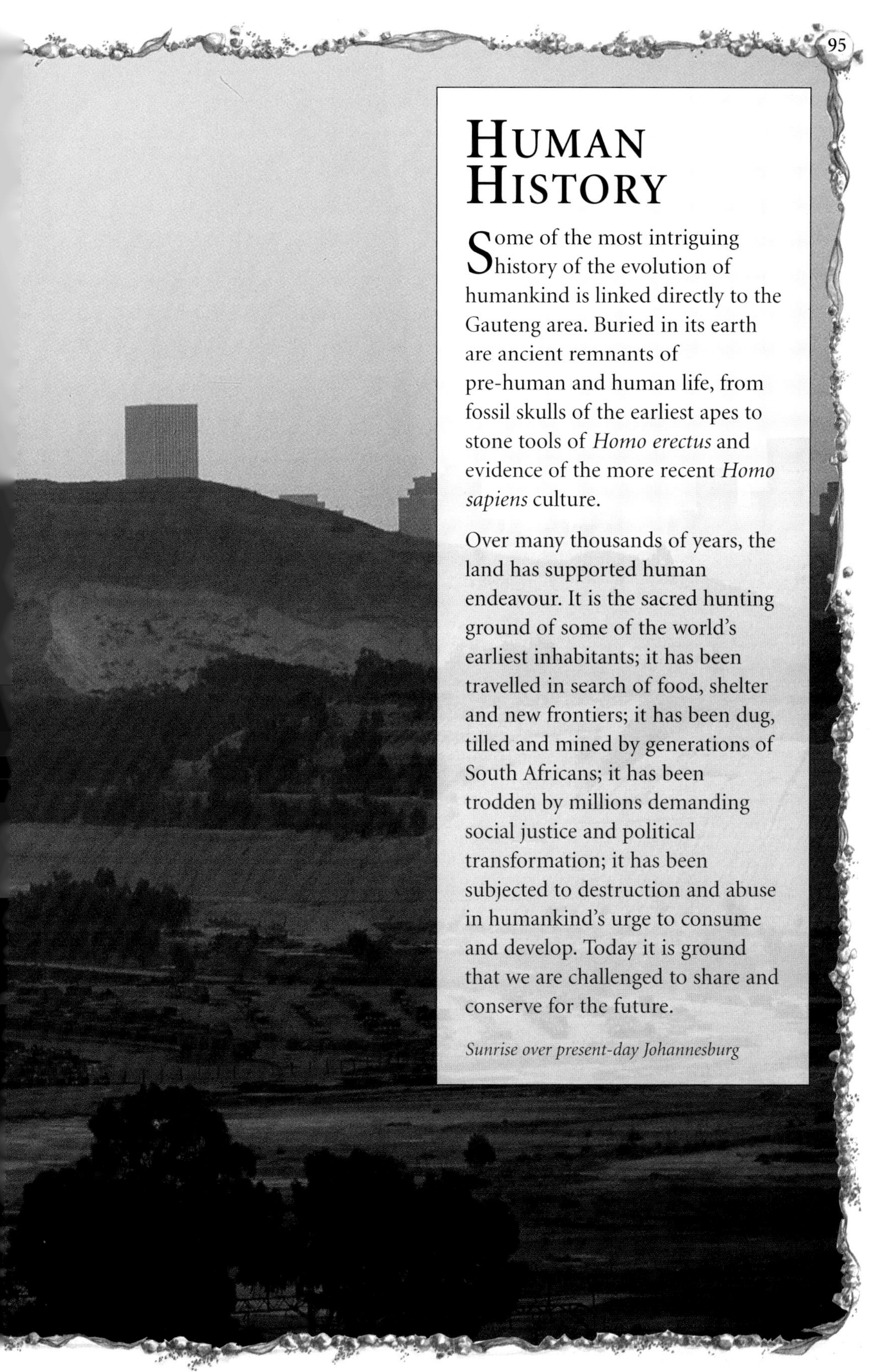

Human History

Some of the most intriguing history of the evolution of humankind is linked directly to the Gauteng area. Buried in its earth are ancient remnants of pre-human and human life, from fossil skulls of the earliest apes to stone tools of *Homo erectus* and evidence of the more recent *Homo sapiens* culture.

Over many thousands of years, the land has supported human endeavour. It is the sacred hunting ground of some of the world's earliest inhabitants; it has been travelled in search of food, shelter and new frontiers; it has been dug, tilled and mined by generations of South Africans; it has been trodden by millions demanding social justice and political transformation; it has been subjected to destruction and abuse in humankind's urge to consume and develop. Today it is ground that we are challenged to share and conserve for the future.

Sunrise over present-day Johannesburg

The Origins of Humans

Three million years ago, a pre-human species of man-like apes was living in the forests of southern and eastern Africa. The first fossil skull of a grassland hominid, *Australopithecus africanus*, was found in a quarry near Taung in the northern Cape in 1924. At the Sterkfontein and Kromdraai Caves in Gauteng many more of these fossils have been discovered.

In December 1998, scientists from the University of the Witwatersrand in Johannesburg found the near-intact skeleton of a 3,5 million-year-old hominid at the Sterkfontein Caves (see grid page 22). The discovery is the most significant in decades, and places South Africa in a unique position on the map of human evolution.

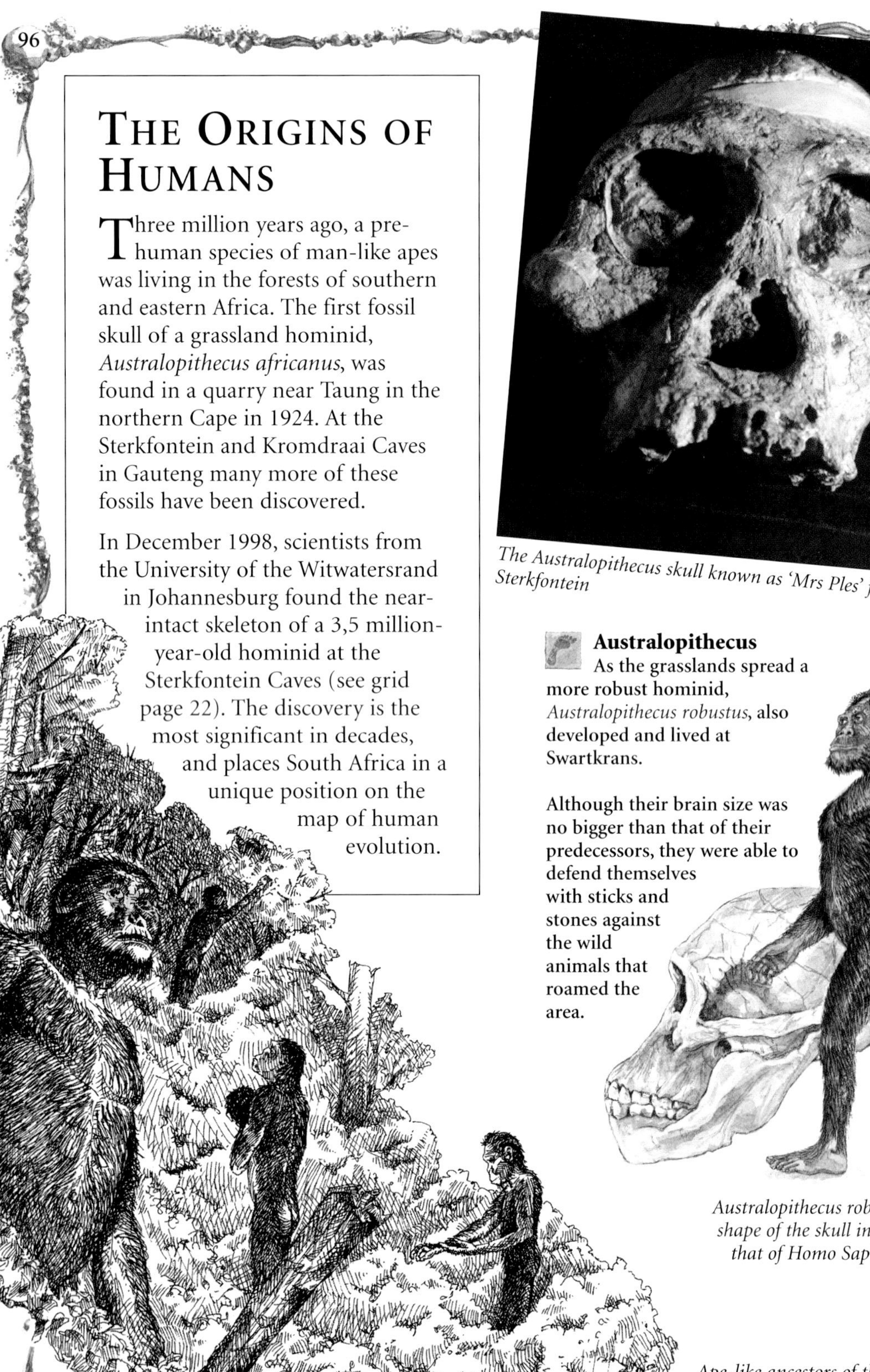

The Australopithecus skull known as 'Mrs Ples' found at Sterkfontein

Australopithecus

As the grasslands spread a more robust hominid, *Australopithecus robustus*, also developed and lived at Swartkrans.

Although their brain size was no bigger than that of their predecessors, they were able to defend themselves with sticks and stones against the wild animals that roamed the area.

Australopithecus robustus. Not[e] shape of the skull in compariso[n] that of Homo Sapiens (on rig[ht]

Ape-like ancestors of the human species lived in forests

Excavation site at Gladysvale, near Sterkfontein Caves

The first tool-making humans were living at Sterkfontein about 1,7 million years ago. Their brain size was larger than that of the man-apes. They made simple stone tools for hunting and digging up roots.

Many of the tools found in the Sterkfontein Caves, for example, are made of quartzite, indicating that the inhabitants were intelligent enough to select the stones most suitable for tools. These early humans were the ancestors of modern humans. Their ability to make stone tools marked the beginning of the Stone Age.

TIME-LINE

The diagram below shows the succession of near-human species leading to modern humans, with a detailed grid of the last 130 000 years.

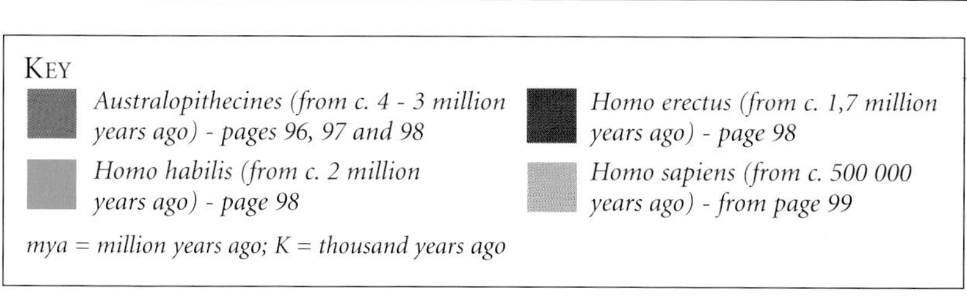

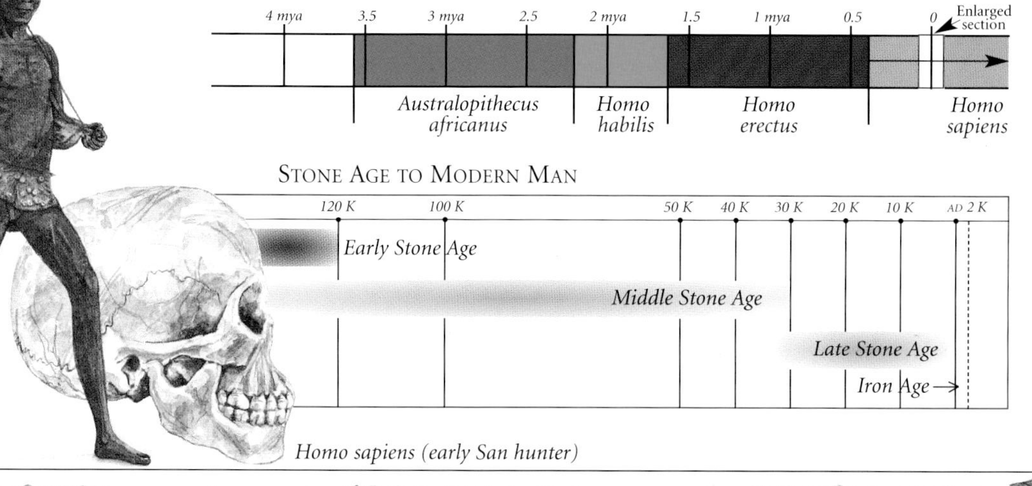

Homo sapiens (early San hunter)

The Stone Age

Sites in the Gauteng area provide evidence of the evolution of humankind from the pre-human australopithecines to people who made more sophisticated stone tools. Fossils discovered during lime mining in the 1930s at Sterkfontein, Swartkrans and Kromdraai near Krugersdorp (see page 22) date back to between about 4 and 1,5 million years ago. The fossils include extinct animals like sabre-toothed cats, and antelope. Australopithecines were the first human ancestors to live outside forests when drier climates encouraged the spread of savannah grasslands.

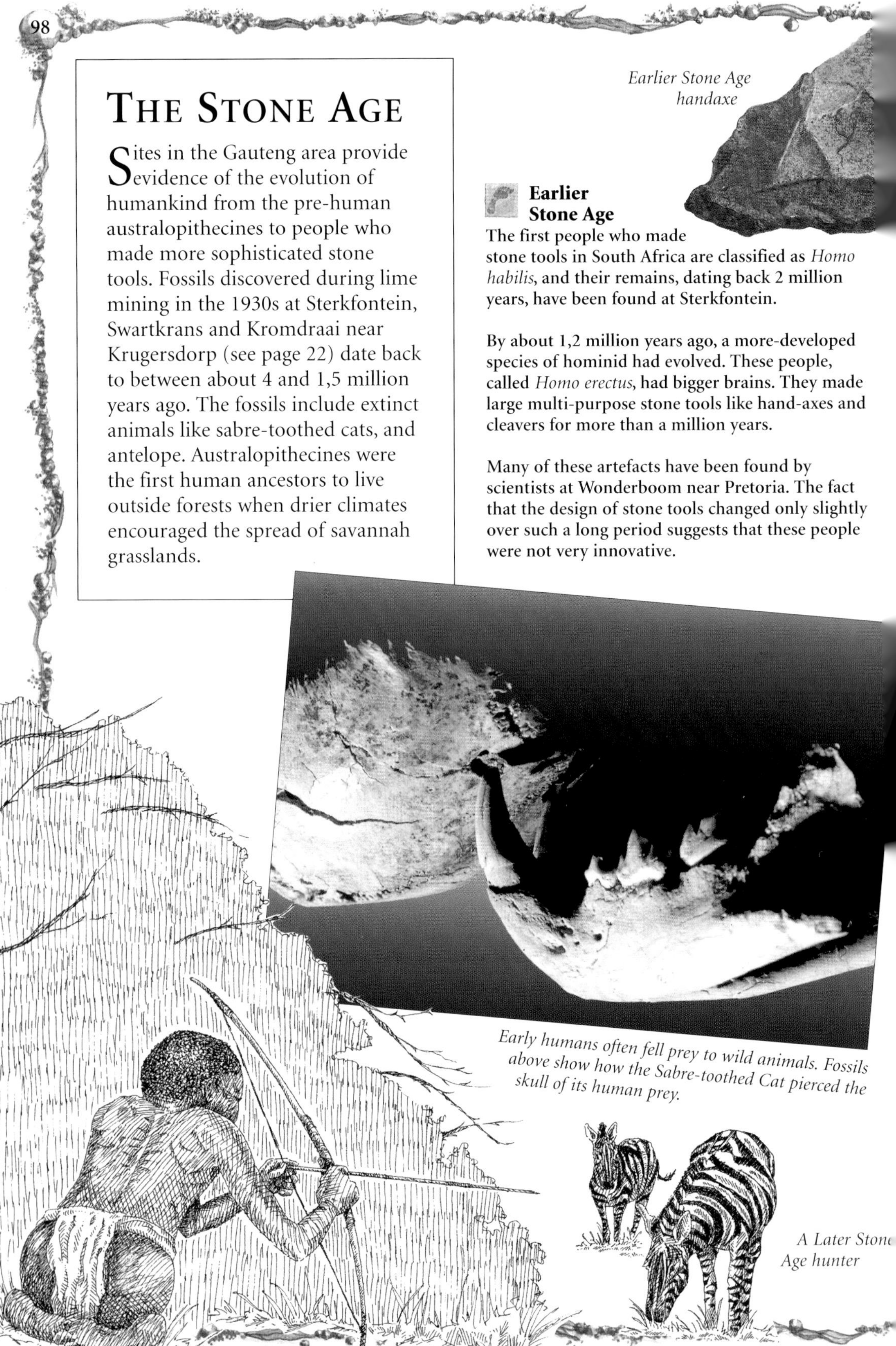

Earlier Stone Age handaxe

Earlier Stone Age

The first people who made stone tools in South Africa are classified as *Homo habilis*, and their remains, dating back 2 million years, have been found at Sterkfontein.

By about 1,2 million years ago, a more-developed species of hominid had evolved. These people, called *Homo erectus*, had bigger brains. They made large multi-purpose stone tools like hand-axes and cleavers for more than a million years.

Many of these artefacts have been found by scientists at Wonderboom near Pretoria. The fact that the design of stone tools changed only slightly over such a long period suggests that these people were not very innovative.

Early humans often fell prey to wild animals. Fossils above show how the Sabre-toothed Cat pierced the skull of its human prey.

A Later Stone Age hunter

Middle Stone Age scraper and blade

...dle Stone Age

...t 200 000 years ago people began making ...er stone tools like scrapers and blades. By this ... they were controlling fire more successfully ... their ancestors, and they lived in caves and ... shelters more often. Stones were also used to ... ochre, which Middle Stone Age people used ...corate their bodies.

...0 000 years ago Middle Stone Age people were ... modern in their appearance. They were ...bers of the species *Homo sapiens*, as are all ...le in the world today.

...rtant Middle Stone Age sites have been found ...nksfield and Primrose in Johannesburg.

The Sterkfontein Caves were once home to Homo habilis.

...r Stone Age

...een 25 000 and 10 000 years ago stone tool ...ing became much more advanced. The bow and ...oned arrow were introduced; arrowheads were ...e of small stone inserts and polished bone ...ts. Ostrich eggshell ornaments, bored stone digging stick weights and various wood tools were made. Examples of such tools have been recovered from several rock shelters in the Magaliesberg.

19th Century San bow and bone-tipped arrow

Rock paintings and rock engravings were an important innovation during the Later Stone Age, and can be seen at several sites (see page 22) and ...useums (see page 24). The art ... an integral part of the belief ...em of the resident people ... San) and their ancestors. ... animals depicted had ...gious significance for ... artists, and human ...res, and abstract ...gns represent ... experiences ...nedicine- ...ple.

Fragments of charcoal and ochre used by the San as pigments

A San paintbrush

San rock painting depicting animals prevalent at the time

The Iron Age

The Iron Age in South Africa began in the 3rd Century AD, more than a thousand years before Europeans landed at Table Bay. Iron Age culture was imported from north of the Limpopo River, and was probably brought by Bantu-speaking ancestors of the Tswana, Sotho, Zulu and Xhosa.

The best-preserved Iron Age village in South Africa, dating back to AD 300-600, was discovered at Broederstroom, near Hartbeespoort Dam. Remains of large Iron Age villages can also be seen in the Rustenberg area and at Pilanesberg.

Wild Sor[...] similar t[...] grown [...] Irc[...]

Iron Age People

They practised mixed agriculture with both crops and livestock. In places with sufficie[...] water and suitable soils they planted crops like sorgh[...] and millet. Cattle, sheep and goats provided the bulk [...] their food in areas where rainfall was less reliable.

The Broederstroom area was probably a centre for ir[...] production. Iron Age people identified many sources [...] iron, tin, copper and other metal ores, and developed [...] ways of smelting and working them.

Smelting (extracting raw iron from the rock) was don[...] charcoal furnaces (clay ovens). Furnaces used for sme[...] iron can also be seen in the Melville Koppies Nature Reserve (see page 26).

Aerial photo of remains of stone walls of an Iron [...] village at Klipriviersberg, near Johannes[...]

Iron Age people at work

A reconstructed forge, used for working iron after smelting

·ry was also produced in the Iron Age period. Clay pots were for brewing beer and storing milk. Clay urns were made to store ·tal remains of important people in the community, for spiritual ·ns.

e-walled villages built by Iron Age Tswana people date back to 1400 AD e Johannesburg area. In the Klipriviersberg Nature Reserve (see page 26) ·h of the city there are remains of over 160 homesteads, consisting of several , a livestock kraal and possibly a grain storage bin.

Copper necklace and earpiece fashioned by Iron Age people

A reconstructed pot typical of those made by Iron Age people in this area

gments of pottery dating back to the Iron Age

Money cowries used for trading

The 19th Century

The 19th Century was a period of expansion, migration and social upheaval. Trade routes were opening up as far east as Maputo and south to the Cape Colony. Trade in copper and ivory was well established. Various clans migrated in and out of the area, including ancestors of the Swazi, Zulu, Pedi, Tswana and Sotho peoples. They came into contact with white explorers, missionaries and, later, the Boer and English settlers. There was greater competition for land and resources, which led to wars and social disruption among the peoples living in the area.

Mfaqane - 1820-1830

The Mfaqane was one of the most significant social upheavals of the 19th Century. Rivalries among chiefs caused division between clans, and ultimately war. The Gauteng and Magaliesberg areas were the scenes of many invasions and battles for control of land.

A famous invasion was led by Zulu chief Mzilikazi, who fled the kingdom of Shaka in Natal with a small but well-trained army. His warriors caused devastation in the Gauteng area, particularly among the resident Pedi and Tswana peoples. After some years Mzilikazi had established a sizeable kingdom.

In 1829 the first European travellers began visiting from the Cape Colony. The earliest were explorers and British missionaries, who introduced Christianity to African people.

Traditional spear and shield used by Zulu warriors

Mzilikazi seated before a group of his warriors (artist: C.

Mzilikazi's warriors in battle gear

Inside an early explorer's wagon (artist: W.J. Burchell)

Great Trek

A Voortrekker bible

:h farmers (Boers) began crossing the Vaal River in the mid-1830s in :h of new frontiers. Their journey took them across some of the most lous and unforgiving terrain in South Africa. Lack of basic resources fresh water and medicines, along with constant danger from wild nals, snakes and scorpions, made survival even more difficult. These ple, the founders of Afrikaner nationalism, became known as the rtrekkers. Their famous journey from the Cape is called the Great Trek.

837 the Boers, led by Hendrik Potgieter, along with their Tswana and qua allies, had virtually destroyed the kingdom of Mzilikazi and driven and his followers north of the Limpopo River into present-day babwe.

; did not, however, bring peace to the area. Conflicts over land continued to de the people. The Boers declared sovereignty over large parts of Gauteng and the galiesberg. African people were denied the right to claim land, and were forced to it back from white 'landowners'. The Boers themselves, divided along both political religious lines, were often at war with one another or with the British during the 1 Century.

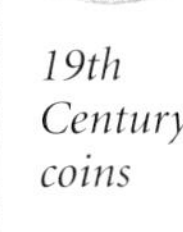

19th Century coins

ortrekkers negotiating perilous terrain

A gold-sifting pan

The Discovery of Gold

Enormous change came to the Gauteng area in the late 1800s. The discovery of gold in 1886 on the farm Langlaagte near present-day Roodepoort marked the beginning of a boom era.

The gold rush brought prosperity and development, as well as a good deal of hard living. Johannesburg grew rapidly into a sizeable town, renowned for its decadence and debauchery.

The Diggers

Diggers arrived in great numbers from all over the country. They found *a des dreary space of open veld over which the bleak winds of winter-time had a passage unhindered and unchecked b presence of any human habitation save a few farmhous*

A mining camp was erected on the site of present-day Commissioner Street, and by September 1886 over 6(prospectors were living there.

News of the gold discovery spread quickly, and soon people were arriving in great numbers from all over t world to seek their fortune.

In a wild, greedy rush they came … on foot, on bicycles, mules, in carts and coaches, even in a hansom cab. Road were few and travelling conditions appalling. Everything to be conveyed by ox-wagon, the teams drawing their gre loads over mountains and across rivers … Soon these ro were strewn with the carcasses of hapless animals which, overcome with hunger, thirst or fatigue, had fallen by the way … to become a whitened skeleton trail leading all th way to the Rand.

F Addington Symonds, *The Johannesburg Story*

Ferreira's mining camp - the beginnings of Johannesburg, 1

Gold prospectors flocked the Gauteng area in th late 180

Gold pouring as it is done today

Mine police were employed to control the workers

er supply soon became a serious problem. Initially diggers
, water from small streams, but these were soon
:aminated owing to lack of sanitation. Later, people began sinking wells,
these also became polluted from seepage. In the mid-1890s only one in
: wells contained water fit for human consumption.

ing changed the landscape of Johannesburg and the surrounding area. Some people
ame extremely wealthy very quickly. Stately homes were built along the northern ridges
resent-day Houghton and Linksfield, and the inner city became a vibrant, though often
adent, metropolis.

: introduction of deep-level mining further increased the population. Thousands of
ican men were recruited from all over South Africa and from neighbouring countries
vork underground for very low wages. They were housed in cramped, segregated and
ctly controlled compounds around Johannesburg.

19th Century miner's lamp

Gold Reef City brings to life the history of early mining in and around Johannesburg

Gold Kruger Rands

The Early 20th Century

Division and conflict among the various peoples of South Africa have dominated the country's social and political landscape during the 20th Century. Struggles have taken place over land and mineral resources, as well as over the racial discrimination that legislated political and economic power in the hands of a minority of the population. Economic development during the 20th Century, however, has helped to make South Africa an industrial powerhouse on the continent.

1899 - 1902

During this period a bloody war was fought for control of the land and resources of the Transvaal (Gauteng). The South African (Second Anglo-Boer) War was the culmination of decades of tension and skirmishes between the British and the Boer nationalists. Remains of stone blockhouses and other fortifications can still be seen in parts of the Magaliesberg, where some famous battles took place.

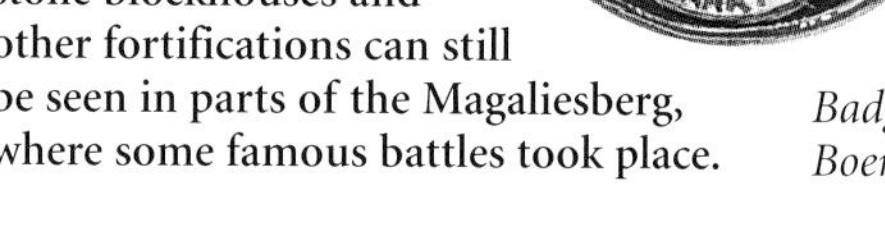

Badge worn Boer soldie

A stone blockhouse in the Magaliesb

Boer and British soldiers in battle

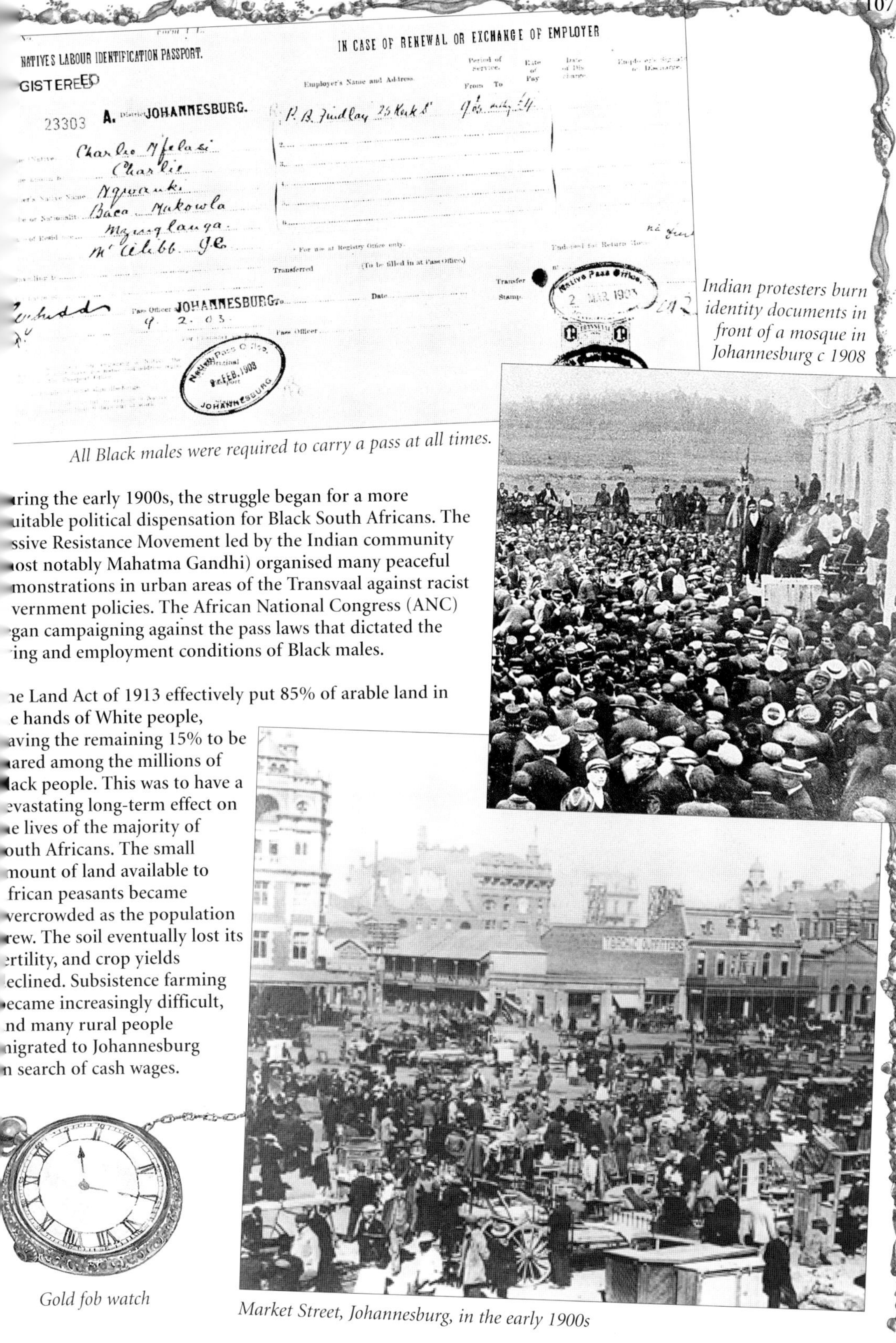

NATIVES LABOUR IDENTIFICATION PASSPORT.

GISTERED

23303 A. District JOHANNESBURG.

Charlie Mfelasi
Charlie
Nqoanki
Baca Makowla
Mzimglanga
M'Cilibb. ge.

Pass Officer JOHANNESBURG
9. 2. 03.

IN CASE OF RENEWAL OR EXCHANGE OF EMPLOYER

Employer's Name and Address.

P. B. Findlay 25 Kerk St

Transferred

(To be filled in at Pass Office.)

Date

Pass Officer

Transfer Stamp.

Native Pass Office
2 MAR 1903

Native Pass Office
Original Passport
9 FEB 1903
JOHANNESBURG

All Black males were required to carry a pass at all times.

Indian protesters burn identity documents in front of a mosque in Johannesburg c 1908

Market Street, Johannesburg, in the early 1900s

Gold fob watch

ıring the early 1900s, the struggle began for a more uitable political dispensation for Black South Africans. The ssive Resistance Movement led by the Indian community ıost notably Mahatma Gandhi) organised many peaceful monstrations in urban areas of the Transvaal against racist vernment policies. The African National Congress (ANC) gan campaigning against the pass laws that dictated the ing and employment conditions of Black males.

ne Land Act of 1913 effectively put 85% of arable land in e hands of White people, aving the remaining 15% to be ıared among the millions of lack people. This was to have a evastating long-term effect on ıe lives of the majority of outh Africans. The small mount of land available to frican peasants became vercrowded as the population rew. The soil eventually lost its ertility, and crop yields eclined. Subsistence farming ecame increasingly difficult, nd many rural people nigrated to Johannesburg n search of cash wages.

1940s to Today

In 1948 the National Party came to power, and over the next 40 years implemented the policy that became known as apartheid. South African society became almost completely polarised as Black people were forcibly removed from the inner cities to outlying townships or to artificially created 'homelands' (bantustans).

Sophiatown

The suburb of Sophiatown in Johannesburg was the scene of one of the more notorious forced removals. Famous in the 1950s as the home of jazz and marabi music, Sophiatown was declared a 'white area' in 1953. One of the most vibrant communities in South Africa was effectively dissolved, and Black residents were forced to move to overcrowded and poorly serviced townships, like Soweto.

Jazz instruments: trumpet and sax mouthpiece

A busy Sophiatown street pr to forced remov

Pro-democracy march

Outside the courthouse during the Rivonia Trial

: policies of apartheid ther fuelled racial tensions ween the peoples of South ica. The legislated racial regation of communities l the unequal distribution and, housing and ication increased poverty l serious social unrest. : country was in crisis several decades.

nificant events in the uggle against apartheid lude the signing of the edom Charter at ptown, Soweto (1956); Sharpeville massacre (1960); the Rivonia Trial, which prominent leaders of the ANC were tenced to life imprisonment for treason; Soweto uprising (1976); and the CODESA gotiations (1991-1993) which led to the first nocratic elections in 1994.

Souvenir badge

1994 inauguration coins

Celebrating in the new South Africa

Human Impact

Humans are able to change their surroundings in ways not available to other species, which must simply adapt to what they find. If humans are to change the environment without damaging it, they need the sensitivity, awareness and responsibility to make sure that the change is always positive, and is brought about only for unselfish reasons. Too often, this does not happen; the environment belongs to all creatures, but only humans treat it unkindly.

Gold nuggets

The Effect of Mining

Mining has changed the face of areas like the Witwatersrand. As mines became deeper, the dumps became higher, and the naturally flat skyline was broken by even-sided, flat-topped, man-made mountains. Miners fro rural areas brought with them the need for home comforts, like open wood- or coal-burning fires. In winter, and of an evening, their smoke coloured the sunsets a deeper purple and orange than ever Nature intended. As more people migrated to the city, infor traders seized the opportunity to provide food and o essentials to the growing numbers.

Mine Dumps

Mine dumps have, since the beginning of the 20th Century, marked the course of the gold-bearing reef along the Witwatersrand. They are piles of finely crushed rock from which the gold has been extracted With improvements in gold extraction techniques, however, many of the older dumps have been re-processed and removed, and a feature of the Witwatersrand (the Reef) is being lost.

Their colour and early lack of vegetation are due to the chemicals used in the extraction process. Only when the poisons, such as cyanide, have been leached from the upper layers, is grass able to take root. In more recent years special exotic trees and grasses ha been planted that tolerate the dump soil better than indigenous types.

Mine dumps, such as this one north-w Johannesburg, are slowly disappea

Informal trading on streets of Johannesbu *(see grid page 2*

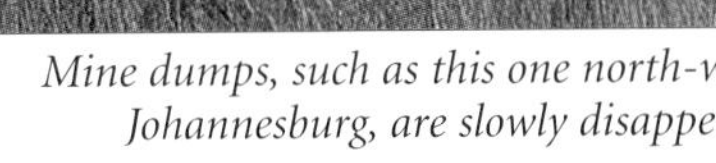

Headgears

ugh they are not as noticeable as mine dumps, the ears are as much a part of the Reef's skyline as any structure. The lift, or skip, used to lower and raise ment, mined rock, and personnel, is suspended a gantry constructed over the opening of a vertical haft. The kilometres of cable needed to reach the m of the shaft are stored on huge drums in a multi- building next to the headgear. Previously, a skip- tor controlled its operation, judging distances, ons and heights, thousands of metres below, using ome gauges and marks painted on the cable. The ss was greatly complicated by the stretch in the which varied depending on the weight in the skip. the computer has made this highly skilled and responsible job obsolete.

Mine headgear

ing Fossil Fuels

mal and lower-income settlements are often poorly ied with adequate power sources. Firewood and although increasingly difficult to obtain, remain the al sources of both warmth and cooking power. The , particularly in winter, is a dense cloud of smog angs over these areas. Air pollution, both within ttlements and of the surrounding areas, is not only htly but also a very serious health hazard. ratory and bronchial illnesses abound, with ren often being the worst affected.

Informal trading is a burgeoning industry.

Informal Trading

In recent years many people have moved into the city in search of work and a better life-style. The city's infrastructure has not been able to accommodate them effectively, nor provide an adequate number of additional jobs. The result is the burgeoning informal trading industry.

Stalls are erected wherever there is space and a sufficient number of potential customers. Goods for sale include prepared food, clothing, curios, refreshments, and fresh farm produce, as well as a range of cosmetic and repair services.

Carved hippo curio

Human Impact

As Gauteng became an increasingly industrialised area, increasing numbers of both skilled and unskilled workers were attracted to the towns and cities. In rural areas, farmers acquired virgin land and changed grasslands to pastures and fields. Fire became an important tool. It quickly cleared unwanted vegetation, but upset natural growth cycles if used unwisely. Nearer the towns, trees planted for shade and decoration began to have a noticeable effect on the environment (see Man-made forests page 69).

Man-made Forest

When urban areas are first settled, people tend to plant trees. One of the biggest urban forests in the world has been planted in and around Johannesburg.

Most of the species are exotics, because in this natural grassland the majority of indigenous tree grow only in specific riverine and rocky habitats. The shelter and food the trees offer was soon identified by birds, and the man-made forest now has a rich and varied birdlife.

The names of some of the older northern suburb reflect a time when trees were probably planted in plantations: Frankenwald (the French Forest), Saxonwold (the English Forest) etc. The trees contribute greatly to the charm of the Johannesburg and Pretoria suburbs.

Man-made forests cover most of Johannesburg's northern su

Jacaranda leaves (see page 69)

Veld fire at Pilanesberg

Veld Fires

Veld fires are characteristic of Gauteng's autumns and winters. Fires are a feature of grasslands the world over, and serve to clear dead, dry grass to make way for the new growth of spring. Farmers wishing to stimulate new grass for early grazing start many of the fires, but if the fires occur too early, the winter cold can harm the grass and cause a delay in the new spring growth. It is best to leave Nature to start the fires, usually by lightning or spontaneous combustion, in her own time.

Farming

Because Gauteng is a natural grassland, early settlers were quick to establish farms. Raising crops and grazing livestock were, and still are, the most common farming activities. Farming ranges from the highly scientific and technologically advanced to subsistence farming, and all have their own impact on the environment. Subsistence farmers are unable to rotate and fertilize their tiny plots adequately, and their crops diminish over time, until they are forced to move on. If they are grazing small herds of livestock, they will often fire the veld to force new growth. The larger, established farmers can afford to fertilise their fields and rotate their crops. They are also able to graze their herds in different fields, and so prevent over-grazing in any one area.

Rooigras
(see page 63)

Helping our environment to survive

- Avoid starting fires in the incorrect season, if at all.
- Recycle your glass, plastic, tins, etc.
- Plant trees and plants indigenous to your area, which also provide nesting places for birds.
- Leave plants, flowers and seeds in their natural environment.
- Never kill, collect or disturb animals and insects.
- Do not pollute the water.
- Do not leave your litter for others to clean up.

...sked ...aver ...page 77)

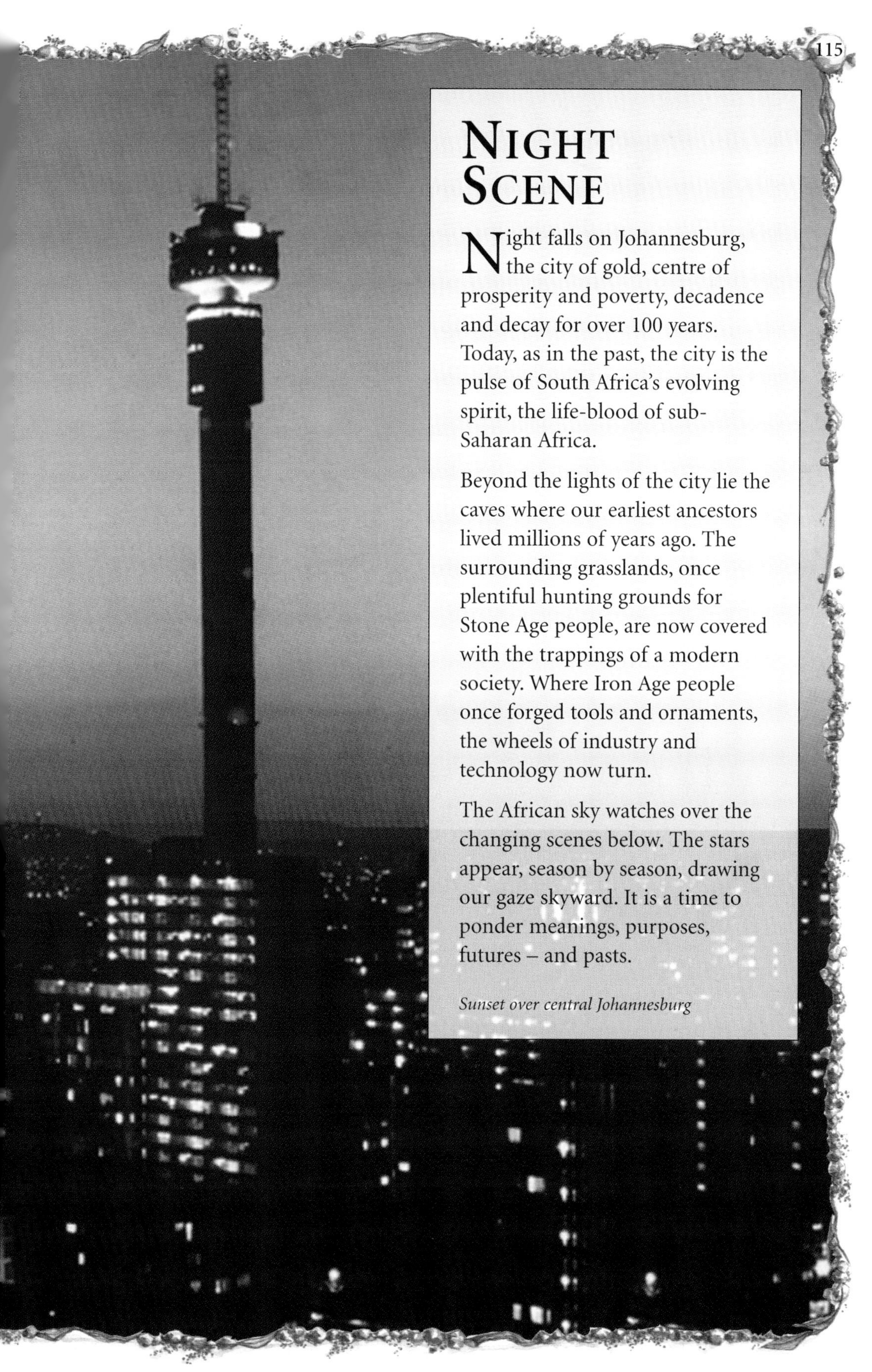

Night Scene

Night falls on Johannesburg, the city of gold, centre of prosperity and poverty, decadence and decay for over 100 years. Today, as in the past, the city is the pulse of South Africa's evolving spirit, the life-blood of sub-Saharan Africa.

Beyond the lights of the city lie the caves where our earliest ancestors lived millions of years ago. The surrounding grasslands, once plentiful hunting grounds for Stone Age people, are now covered with the trappings of a modern society. Where Iron Age people once forged tools and ornaments, the wheels of industry and technology now turn.

The African sky watches over the changing scenes below. The stars appear, season by season, drawing our gaze skyward. It is a time to ponder meanings, purposes, futures – and pasts.

Sunset over central Johannesburg

Index

Abeiling 20
Acacia caffra 61
Acacia karroo 61, 67
Acacia mearnsii 70
Acacia robusta robusta 61
Acacia tortilis 61
Acacia, Brack Thorn 61
 Broad-pod Splendid 61
 Common Hook-thorn 61
 Sweet -thorn **61**, 67
 Umbrella 61
Acherontia atropos 56
Acinonyx jubatus 90
Aepyceros melampus 87
Aeshnidae family 57
African Fish Eagle 44, **83**
African Honey Bee 56
African Monarch Butterfly 57
African National Congress **109**, 111
Afrikaner nationalism 105
African Olive 64
African White-stinkwood 68
Agama aculeata 48
Agama, Ground 48
Agriculture 102
Air adventure 20
Air flips 20
Air pollution 113
Alcelaphus buselaphus 89
Aloe davyana (greatheadii) 56
Aloe marlothii 59
Aloe, Mountain 59
 Spotted 56
Alopochen aegyptiacus 82
Amphibians 44
Anas undulata 82
Anglo-Boer War, Second 108
Anhinga melanogaster 82
Animals, captive 25
Annual Cultural Festivals 20
Ant, Velvet 54
Antelope, Sable 89
Aonyx capensis 91
Apartheid 110, 111
Aphid 56
Aphididae 56
Apis mellifera adansonii 56
Apus caffer 75
Aquila verreauxii 75
Ardea melanocephala 81
Arrowheads 101
Astronomy 21
Australopithecines **97**, 98, 99, 100
Australopithecus africanus 98
Australopithecus robustus 98

Baboon, Chacma 93
Banded Tilapia 44
Bantu 102
Bantustans 110
Barbel 44
Barbet, Black-collared 76
 Crested 76
 Pied 60
Basement Granite **29**, 31
Bat, Cape Serotine 93
Bee, African Honey 56
Bee-eater, White-fronted 78
Beer 103
Beetle, Rose 64
Belonogaster species 54
Besembossie 53
Bidens formosa 52
Bidens pilosa 54
Big Five 87, 90
Bird sanctuaries 15
Birdwatching 15
Birding 15
Birds 73
Bishop, Red 80
Bitis arietans 47
Black Eagle **75**, 92
Black Reef 30, 31, 32
Black Rhinoceros 87
Black Wattle 70
Black-backed Jackal 91
Black-collared Barbet 64, 76
Black-eyed Bulbul 78
Black-headed Heron 81
Blackjack 54
Black-shouldered Kite 75
Bladder-nut, Inland 67
Bloodwood, Kiaat 40
Blades 101
Blue Guarri 66
Blue Kurper 44
Blue Wildebeest 89
Bluebush,Karoo 67
Bluebush, Star-apple 67
Boers 104, 105, 108
Bostrychia hagedash 74
Botanical gardens 25
Botterblom 54
Bow and arrow 101
Braamfonteinspruit 35
Brachylaena rotundata 62
Brack Thorn Acacia 61
Brazilian Verbena 52
British colonialism 104, 105, 108
Broad-pod Splendid Acacia 61
Broederstroom 102
Brown Hyaena 91
Brown-hooded Kingfisher 83
Browsers 92
Bubo africanus 77
Bubulcus ibis 81
Buddleja, Olive 59
Buddleja saligna 59
Buffalo-thorn Jujube 63
Bugweed 71
Bulbul, Black-eyed 78
Bullfrog 45
Bungee jumping 20
Burchell's Zebra 89
Burial 103
Bushbaby, Lesser 61, **92**
Bushwillow, River 60
 Velvet-leaved 60
Buteo buteo 75
Butterfly, African Monarch 57
Buzzard, Steppe 75

Cabbage Tree, Highveld 41, 51, **59**
 Mountain 41, 51, **59**
Caco, Common 45
Cacosternum boettgeri 45
Canary Weed 53
Canis mesomelas 91
Canoeing 19
Cape Clawless Otter 91
Cape Colony ('the Cape') 104
Cape Dwarf Gecko 48
Cape Robin 79
Cape Serotine Bat 93
Cape Skink 48
Cape Sparrow 80
Cape Vulture 74
Cape Wagtail 79
Cape White-eye 65, **78**
Captive animals 25
Cardinal Woodpecker 76
Carissa bispinosa 68
Carnivores 90
Carrion Flower, Giant 57
Cassia mimosoides 54
Cassia, Fishbone 54
Catfish, Sharp-toothed 44
Cattle Egret 81
Cave-dwellers 101
Caves, dolomite 34
Celtis africana 68
Centipede 65
Ceratotheca triloba 55
Ceratotherium simum 88
Cercopithecus aethiops 93
Ceryle rudis 83
Chacma Baboon 93
Chafer, Fruit 64
Chamaeleo dilepis 48
Chameleon, Flap-neck 48
Cheetah 90
Chilopoda class 65
Chiromantis xerampeliua 45
Christianity 104
Cicada 69
Cicadidae family 69
Clarias gariepinus 44
Clawed Toad 45
Clay 102, 103
Cleaver 100
Climate 100
Climbing 20
Cobra, Egyptian 46
 Mozambique Spitting 46
 Snouted 46
Coccinellidae family 56
CODESA 111
Coenagrionidae family 57
Columba guinea 81
Combretum erythrophyllum 60
Combretum molle 60
Commissioner Street 106

on Brown Water Snake 67
on Caco 45
on Currant-rhus 67
on Duiker 86
on Hook-thorn Acacia 61
on Platanna 45
on Reed 57
on River Frog 45
on Spikethorn 65
on Sugarbush 62
on Wild Currant 67
on Wild Pear 62
nsation Level 38
chaetes taurinus 89
Red-knobbed 83
r 102, 104
ush 60
rant, Reed 82
albus 74
aixoides concolor 77
s 52
ha caffra 79
don orbiculata 54
ry clubs 18
River 49
d Barbet 76
t 69
t, King 69
n bulbispermum 53
dile River 35
berry, Raisin 58
n gratissimus 68
n, Lavender 68
Pied **74**, 91
ned Plover 81
o, Red-chested 79
us solitarius 76
Mosquito 69
quinquefasciata 69
ral festivals 20
s 21
nt, Common Wild 67
nt-rhus, Common 67
nia paniculata 59
us rupestris 65

chick 83
a, Wild 55
s 25
selfly 57
aus chrysippus 57
er 82
ie 75, 90, **92**
peltis scabra 46
h's Head Hawk Moth 56
dropicos fuscescens 76
rmekaar Stamperwood 66
39
ros bicornis 87
rostachys cinerea 60
ging sticks 101
pyros lycioides 67
pyros whyteana 67
opoda class 65
mite caves 34
nbeya rotundifolia 62
Dombeya, Wild-pear 62
Dove, Laughing 79
Dragonfly 57
Duck, Yellow-billed 82
Duiker, Common 86
Dung Beetle 64
Dutch farmers, see Boers
Dwarf Gecko, Cape 48
Dwarf Sedge 65

Eagle, African Fish 44, **83**
Black **75**, 92
Eagle Owl, Spotted 77
Earlier Stone Age 99, 100
Early humans 97-101
Eco-Tourist Accommodation 16
Egg-eater, Rhombic 46
Egret, Cattle 81
Egyptian Cobra 46
Egyptian Goose 82
Ehretia rigida 66
Eland 86
Elanus caeruleus 75
Elephant 87
Elionurus muticus 63
Emergency telephone numbers 13
Englerophytum magalismontanum 58
English settlers 104
Eptesicus capensis
Equus quagga antiquorum 93
Eucalyptus 70
Euclea crispa 66
Euplectes orix 80
Euplectes progne 80
Europeans 102
Evolution 97, 98, 99, 100, 101
Exotic species 114
Explorers 104

False Olive 59
Farming 109, 115
Fever-berry, Lavender 68
Fine-leaved Verbena 52
Fire 101, 115
Fiscal Shrike 76
Fish Eagle, African 44, **83**
Fish 44
Fishbone Cassia 54
Fishing 16
Flap-neck Chameleon 48
Flea markets 21
Flips, air 20
Flowers 52
Foam Nest Frog 45
Foreign exchange 13
Forest Num-num 68
Forest-dwellers 98, 100
Forests, man-made 69, 114
Fossils 97, 98, 100
Foxglove, Wild 55
Frankenwald 114
Freedom Charter 111
Freezing Level 38
Frogs 45
Bullfrog 45
Common Caco Frog 45
Common River Frog 45
Foam Nest Frog 45
Grey Tree Frog 45
Frost 39
Fruit Chafer 64
Fuels, fossil 113
Fulica cristata 83
Furnaces 103

Galago moholi 92
Galerella sanguinea 91
Game parks/reserves 27
Game viewing 14
Gandhi, Mahatma 109
Gazania krebsiana 54
Gazania 54
Gecko, Cape Dwarf 48
Gemsbok 89
Genet, Small-spotted 91
Genetta genetta 91
Geochelone pardalis 49
Giant Carrion Flower 57
Giant Kingfisher 83
Giant Sedge 57
Gifbol 55
Giraffa camelopardalis 87
Giraffe 87
Gladysvale 99
Glossy Starling 78
Gold Reef City 107
Discovery of 106
Extraction of 112
Gold, origin of 31
Gold-bearing reef 30, 31, 106, 112
Golf courses 18
Gondwana 29
Goose, Egyptian 82
Goose, Spur-winged 82
Grasses 63
Natal Red Top Grass 63
Rooigras 63
Spear Grass 63
Thatch Grass 63
Wire Grass 63
Grasslands 32, 62, 80, 100, 115
Grazers 92
Great Trek, The 105
Grebe, Little 83
Grewia occidentalis 58
Grey Lourie 60, **77**
Grey Tree Frog 45
Grillidae family 69
Griquas 105

Stamvrug Milkplum (page 58)

Ground Agama 48
Guarri, Blue 66
Guineafowl, Helmeted 80
Gymnosporia buxifolia 65
Gyps coprotheres 74

Hadeda Ibis 74
Hail 38
Hairy Senecio 53
Halcyon albiventris 83
Haliaeetus vocifer 83
Hamerkop 39
Handaxe 100
Hartbeespoort Dam 35, 102
Hartebeest, Red 85, **89**
Hawk Moth, Death's Head 56
Helmeted (Marsh) Terrapin 49
Helmeted Guineafowl 80
Hemachatus haemachatus 46
Herbivores 92-95
Heron, Black-headed 81
Heteropogon contortus 63
Highveld Cabbage Tree 41, 51, **59**
Highveld Protea 62
Hiking 17
Hinged Tortoise, Bell's 47
Hippopotamus amphibius 88
Hippopotamus 88
Hippotragus niger 89
Hirundo abyssinica 75
Historical sites 23
Homelands 110
Hominids 98-100
Homo erectus 97, 99, 100
Homo habilis 99, 100
Homo sapiens 97, 99, 101
Hook-thorn Acacia, Common 61
Hook-lipped Rhinoceros 87
Hoopoe 79
Horse performances 16
Horse racing 19
Horse riding 16
Houghton 107
Huernia hystrix 57
Huernia, Porcupine 57
Human history 97
Hunters 90
Hunting 100
Hut dwellings 103
Hyaena brunnea 91
Hyaena, Brown 91
Hydrothermal Theory 31
Hyparrhenia anamesa 63
Hypoxis hemerocallidea 55
Hyrax, Rock 92
Hystrix africaeaustralis 92

Impala 87
Indigenous vegetation 14
Industry, South African 108
Informal trading, see Trading
Information centres 12
Inland Bladder-nut 67
Insects 51, 56, 69
Invasions 104
Ipomoea bathycolpos 55
Ipomoea bolusiana 55
Ipomoea crassipes 55
Ipomoea magnusiana 55
Ipomoea ommaneyi 55
Ipomoea transvaalensis 55
Iron Age 102
Iron 102
Ivory 104

Jacaranda mimosifolia 69
Jacaranda 69
Jackal, Black-backed 91
Jacket-plum 64
Jazz music 110
Jewellery 103
Johannesburg 97, 98, 101, 102, 110, 114
  Early history of 106, 107, 109
Jukskei River 35
Jujube, Buffalo-thorn 63

Karee 67
Karee, Mountain 67
Karee-rhus, Rocky 67
Karoo Bluebush 67
Kayaking 19
Kiaat Bloodwood 40
Kiggelaria africana 65
King Cricket 69
Kingfisher, Brown-hooded 83
Kingfisher, Giant 83
Kingfisher, Pied 83
Kinixys belliana 47
Kite, Black-shouldered 75
Kite, Yellow-billed 74
Klipriviersberg Nature Reserve 102, 103
Kliptown 111
Kloofs 33
Kobus ellipsiprymnus 88
Kromdraai Caves 98, 100
Krugersdorp 100
Kudu 86
Kurper, Blue 44

Labeo rosae 44
Ladybird 56
Lakes, smaller 25
Lamprotornis nitens 78
Land Act of 1913 109
Land ownership 105
Langlaagte 106
Lanius collaris 76
Lantana camara 56
Lantana 56
Later Stone Age 99-101
Laughing Dove 79
Laurasia 29
Lavender Croton 68
Lavender Fever-berry 68
Leonatis leonuris 55
Leopard Tortoise 49
Leopard 44, **90**
Lesser Bushbaby 92
Lesser-striped Swallow 75
Leucosidea sericea 63
Lightning 39
Lily, Orange River 53
Limpopo River 102, 105
Linksfield 101, 107
Lion 90
Little Grebe 83
Long-legged birds 81
Long-tailed Widow 80
Lourie, Grey 77
Loxodonta africana 87
Lycodonomorphus rufulus 47
Lybius torquatus 76
Lygodactylus capensis 48

Mabuya capensis 48
Magaliesberg 32, 33, 35, 101, 104, 108
Mammals 85
Mankwe Dam 29
Man-made forests 69, 114
Mantis, Praying 48
Maputo 104
Mariscus congestus 57
Market Street, Johannesburg 109
Marsh Terrapin 49
Marula 58
Masked Weaver **77**, 115
Mason Wasp 54
Medicinal and poisonous flowers
Medicine people 101
Medlar, Wild 63
Megaceryle maxima 83
Melia azedarach 70
Melinis repens 63
Melville Koppies Nature Reserve 1
Merops bullockoides 78
Mfaqane 104
Middle Stone Age 99, 101
Migration to Johannesburg 107, 1
  113
Milk 103
Milkplum, Stamvrug 58
  Transvaal 58
Millet 102
Millipede 65
Milvus migrans parasitus 74
Minaret Flower 55
Mine compounds 107
Mine dumps 112
Mine headgears 113
Mine workers, African 107
  recruitment of 107
Mining, deep-level 107
  Gold 107
  History of 106, 107, 113
Missionaries 104
Mole Snake 47
Mongoose, Slender 91
Monitor, Nile 49
  Rock 49
Monkey, Vervet 75, **93**
Monkey's Tail 52
Monuments 23
Morning Glory 55
Mosquito, Culex 69
Motacilla capensis 79
Moth, Death's Head Hawk 56
Mountain Aloe 59

in biking 16
in building 32
in Cabbage Tree 51, **59**
in Karee 67
in Silver-oak 62
Striped 75
ird, Red-faced 77
bique Spitting Cobra 46
bique Tilapia 44
s 98
ı, Red-nosed 44
lea sericea 60
pal substructures 12
ns 24
dae family 54
zi 104, 105

nnulifera 46
ossambica 46
104
Red Top Grass 63
al Party 110
l History sites 22
reserves 26, 102
inia talatala 77
activities 21
onitor 49
la meleagris 80
num, Forest 68

9
Mountain Silver 62
101
rus species 54
ood 63
uropaea 64
Sagewood 59
Thrush 79
African 64
Wild 64
ognathus morio 81
ge River Lily 53
hromis mossambicus 44
ns of humans 98-101
nents 101
gazella 89
h eggshell ornaments 101
s lanceolata 68
Cape Clawless 91
ut 63
Spotted Eagle 77

yderms 86
ea 29
hera leo 90
hera pardus 90
r Wasp 54
ursinus 93
ea capensis 64
s 27
own Prawn 69
laws 109
r melanurus 80
ve Resistance Movement 109
n, Wild 65
Common Wild 62

Pedi 104
Pelomedusa subrufa 49
Phacochoerus aethiopicus 92
Phalacrocorax africanus 82
Phragmites australis 57
Pied Barbet 60
Pied Crow **74**, 91
Pied Kingfisher 83
Piet-my-vrou 76
Pigeon, Rock 81
Pilanesberg 29, 37, 102
Pine 71
Pioneer plants 52, 63
Placer Theory 31
Plains Zebra 89
Plakkie 54
Plants 51
Platanna, Common 45
Plectropterus gambensis 82
Ploceus velatus 77
Plover, Crowned 81
Plumbago 53
Plumbago auriculata 53
Pony riding 16
Poplar 71
Porcupine Huernia 57
Porcupine 92
Potgieter, Hendrik 105
Potomonautes perlatus 49
Pottery 103
Praying Mantis 48
Pre-human life 97, 98
Pretoria 114
Primrose 101
Procavia capensis 92
Protea caffra 62
Protea Highveld 62
Psammophylax rhombeatus 47
Pseudaspis cana 47
Puffadder 47
Puzzle Bush 66
Pycnonotus barbatus 78
Pyxicephalus adspersus 45

Quartz and quartzite 31, 99
Quercus robur 69

Racial discrimination 108-111
Railway trips 13
Rain 38
Rainfall records 41
Raisin, Cross-berry 58
Rana angolensis 45
Rand, see Witwatersrand
Raptors 75
Red Bishop 80
Red Hartebeest 85, **89**
Red Toad 45
Red-chested Cuckoo 76
Red-faced Mousebird 77
Red-knobbed Coot 83
Red-nosed Mudfish 44
Red-winged Starling 81
Reed Cormorant 82
Reed, Common 57
Reef, the 112, 113

Reptiles 46
Rhabdomys pumilio 75
Rhinoceros, Black/Hook-lipped 87
White/Square-lipped 88
Rhombic Egg-eater 46
Rhombic Skaapsteker 47
Rhus lancea 67
Rhus leptodictya 67
Rhus pyroides 67
Rinkhals 46
River Bushwillow 60
River Crab 49
River Frog, Common 45
River rafting 19
Rivers, craters and caves 34
Rivonia trial 111
Robin, Cape 79
Rock climbing 20
Rock engravings 101
Rock Hyrax 92
Rock Monitor 49
Rock paintings 101
Rock Pigeon 81
Rock Tannin-bush 68
Rocky Karee-rhus 67
Roodepoort 106
Rooigras 63
Rose Beetle 64
Ruminants 92
Rustenburg 37, 102

Sable Antelope 89
Sabre-toothed Cat 100
Sagewood, Olive 59
Sagittarius serpentarius 81
Salix hybrid 71
San 99, 101
Savannah 100
Saxonwold 114
Scarabaeidae family 64
Scavengers 74, 91
Scenic train trips 13
Schisinaderma carens 45
Sclerocarya birrea 58
Scraper 101
Secretary Bird 81
Sedge, Dwarf 65
Giant 57
Seed dispersal 40, 41
Senecio achilleifolius 53
Senecio consanguineus 53
Senecio coronatus 53
Senecio glanduloso-pilosus 53
Senecio inaequidens 53

Glossy Starling (page 78)

Senecio oxyriifolius 53
Senecio venosus 53
Senecio, Hairy 53
Service providers 12
Sesmylspruit 35
Settlers 104
Shaka 104
Sharpeville massacre 111
Sharp-toothed Catfish 44
Shrike, Fiscal 76
Sickle-bush, Small-leaved 60
Silver-oak, Mountain 62
Skaapsteker, Rhombic 47
  Spotted 47
Skink, Cape 48
Slender Mongoose 91
Slootopdammer 53
Smaller lakes 25
Small-leaved Sickle-bush 60
Small-spotted Genet 91
Smelting 102
Snakes 46, 47
  Common Brown Water Snake 47
  Egyptian Cobra 46
  Mole Snake 47
  Mozambique Spitting Cobra 46
  Rhombic Egg Eater 46
  Rinkhals 46
  Snouted Cobra 46
Solanum mauritianum 71
Songololo 65
Sophiatown 110
Sorghum, Wild 102
Sotho 102, 104
South African War 108
Soweto 110, 111
Sparrow, Cape 80
Spear Grass 63
Sphodromantis gastrica 48
Spikethorn, Common 65
Spotted Aloe 56
Spotted Eagle Owl 77
Spotted Skaapsteker 47
Spur-winged Goose 82
Square-lipped Rhinoceros 88
Stamperwood, Deurmekaar 66
Stamvrug Milkplum 58
Stapelia gigantea 57
Star-apple, Bluebush 67
Star Flower 55
Star-gazing 21
Starling, Glossy 78
  Red-winged 81
Stenopelmatidae family 69
Steppe Buzzard 75
Sterkfontein Caves 34, 98-100
Stinkwood, African-white 68, 74
Stone Age 99-101
Stone tools 97-101
Street trading 21
Streptopelia senegalensis 79
Striped Mouse 75
Suikerbosrand Nature Reserve 51
Sumach, Transvaal 68
Sunbird, Whitebellied 77
Summer-flowering plants 52
Sunshine records 41
Swallow, Lesser-striped 75
Swartkrans 98, 100
Swazi 104
Sweet-thorn Acacia **61**, 67
Swift, White-rumped 75
Sybossie 53
Sylvicapra grimmia 86
Symonds, F. Addington 106
Syringa 70

Table Bay 102
Tachybaptus ruficollis 83
Tannin-bush, Rock 68
Taung 98
Taurotragus oryx 86
Temperature records 41
Terrapin, Helmeted 49
Thatch Grass 63
Themeda triandra 63
Thrush, Olive 79
Thunder 39
Tilapia sparrmanii 44
Tilapia, Banded 44
Tilapia, Mozambique 44
Tin 102
Toads 45
  Clawed Toad 45
  Common Platanna 45
  Red Toad 45
Tortoise, Leopard 49
Tour companies 13
Trachyphonus vaillantii 76
Trading, informal 113
Traditionally used trees 60
Tragelaphus strepsiceros 86
Train trips 13
Transport and travel 13
Transvaal Milkplum 58
Transvaal Sumach 68
Transvaal 108, 109
Travel operators 13
Trees 58
Tswaing Crater 36
Tswaing Enviro-museum 36
Tswana 102-105
Turdus olivaceus 79
Turf clubs 19

Umbrella Acacia 61
Unique and striking features 58
University of the Witwatersrand 98
Upupa epops 79
Urban forest, see Forests
Urocolius indicus 77

Vaal River 105
Vanellus coronatus 81
Vangueria infausta 63
Varanus exanthematicus albigularis 49
Varanus niloticus 49
Vegetation zones 40
Vegetation, indigenous 14
Vehicle hire 13
Veldsambreeltjie 55
Velvet Ant 54
Velvet-leaved Bushwillow 60
Velvet Wild-medlar 63
Verbena brasiliensis 52
Verbena tenuisecta 52
Verbena, Brazilian 52
  Fine-leaved 52
Vervet Monkey 75, 93
Viewing, Game 14
Voortrekkers 105
Vulture, Cape 74
Vultures 91

Wagtail, Cape 79
Warning colours 56
Wars 104, 105, 108
Warthog 92
Wasp, Mason 54
  Paper 54
Water birds 82
Waterbuck 88
Water snake, Common Brown 47
Watersports 19
Wattle, Black 70
Weaver, Masked **77**, 115
Wetlands 57
White-bellied Sunbird 77
White-eye, Cape 78
White-fronted Bee-eater 78
White-rumped Swift 75
White Rhinoceros 87
White Stinkwood 68, 98
White-stinkwood, African 68
Widow, Long-tailed 80
Wild Currant, Common 67
Wild Dagga 55
Wild Foxglove 55
Wild-medlar, Velvet 63
Wild Morning Glory 55
Wild Olive 64
Wild-peach 65
Wild-pear Dombeya 62
Wild Pear, Common 62
Wild Sorghum 102
Wild Sweet Potato 55
Wildebeest, Blue 89
Willow 71
Wire Grass 63
Witwatersrand 32, 35, 106, 112
Wonderboom 100
Wood tools 101
Woodpecker, Cardinal 76

***X**enopus laevis* 45
Xerophyta retinervis 52
Xhosa 102

Yachting 19
Yellow-billed Duck 82
Yellow-billed Kite 74

Zebra, Plains (Burchell's) 89
Zimbabwe 105
Ziziphus mucronata 63
Zoological gardens 25
Zosterops pallidus 78
Zulu 102, 104

ACKNOWLEDGEMENTS

Without the combined energy and commitment of the following people, the creation of **Discover the Magic – Gauteng** would not have been possible.

Design

Jacana

Artwork

Lisl Barry
Sally MacLarty
Penny Noall
Mike Parkin
Heidi Streitberger
Joan van Gogh

Photography

Dr Jannette Deacon
Robert de Jonge
Prof. Huffman
Andrew Mohammed
Barry Pohl
Peter Thomas
Gary van der Merwe
Gus van Dyk
Anthony Bannister Photo Library
Bailey's African History Archives
Department of Archaeology University of Witwatersrand
Gauteng Provincial Government
Museum Africa
PictureNET Africa (www.picturenet.co.za)
Unifoto International

DTP Origination

Lynda Ward
Jacana

Map Development

Carto Graphics

Text Development

Dr Jannette Deacon
Lana du Croq
Ivan Ginsberg
Ashley Heron
Gary van der Merwe
Jacana

Text Editors, Checking and Evaluation

Marius Burger
Dr Jannette Deacon
Ivan Ginsberg
Owen Hendry
Geoff Lockwood - Birdlife South Africa
Dr John Manning, Lizette Engelbrecht - National Botanical Institute
Mike Pendrith - Pretoria Zoo
Dr N Rautenbach, Dr P Balis, Dr M Whiting, Alan Kemp - Transvaal Museum
Jacana

Jacana Team

We are proud to acknowledge the work of the entire Jacana team who have contributed in their specialised fields to produce **Discover the Magic – Gauteng:**

Lisl Barry, Janet Bartlet, Carol Broomhall, Tracey Fisher, Joanne Forbes, Ingrid Glashoff, Ashwell Glasson, Ryan Francois, Dr Rina Grant, Clare Kerchhoff, Joanne Mallet, Andrea Meeson, Obed Molobe, Fortune Ncube, Davidson Ndebele, Jannett Ndebele, David Ngwenya, Sue Nel, Bambi Nunes, Jenny Prangley, Zamila Rayman, Joan Sibiya, Mariette Strydom, Amanda Thoane, Peter Thomas, Val Thomas, Camilla Thomas, Pamela Thompson, Gary van der Merwe, Liz van Niekerk

NOTES